Derek Fell's
Handy Garden Guides
perennials

Derek Fell's
Handy Garden Guides

perennials

Growing & design tips
for 200 favorite flowers

FRIEDMAN/FAIRFAX

P U B L I S H E R S

A FRIEDMAN/FAIRFAX BOOK

© 1992, 1996 by Michael Friedman Publishing Group, Inc.

Library of Congress Cataloging-in-Publication data available upon request.

ISBN 1-56799-374-5

Editor: Dana Rosen
Art Director: Jeff Batzli
Designer: Tanya Ross-Hughes
Photography Director: Christopher C. Bain
Cover Design: Jeff Batzli and Maria Mann
All photographs © Derek Fell

Typeset by Bookworks Plus
Color separations by Bright Arts Pte Ltd
Printed in Singapore by KHL Printing Co Pte Ltd

Originally published as
The American Garden Association's Garden Guide to Perennials.

For bulk purchases and special sales, please contact:
Friedman/Fairfax Publishers
Attention: Sales Department
15 West 26th Street
New York, New York 10010
212/685-6610   FAX 212/685-1307

Visit the Friedman/Fairfax Website:
http://www.webcom.com/friedman

Acknowledgments

The author wishes to thank Peggy Fisher for help with research, Kathy Nelson for help with typing the manuscript, Wendy Fields for help with picture selections, and Carolyn Heath for help with styling some of the floral compositions.

CONTENTS

PERENNIALS: YEARLY COLOR

WHAT IS A PERENNIAL?

Plants can be divided into two basic groups: herbaceous plants, or plants that grow soft stems, and woody plants, those with a more durable cell structure. The latter group includes trees and shrubs. The former group includes annuals, biennials, and perennials. Annuals complete their life cycle, from seed germination to seed dispersal, in one year. Biennials complete their life cycle in two years; they grow a healthy crown of leaves the first year and flower and set seed the second. Perennials are similar to biennials, but instead of dying the second year, they continue living from year to year.

The broad classification of perennials is divided into several groups. Some perennials survive harsh winters and are called hardy perennials; others cannot tolerate freezing winters and are referred to as tender perennials. Some perennials survive a period of dormancy by means of an underground bulbous storage organ; these are generally referred to as flowering bulbs. Those that survive by roots are considered true perennials, but since a small number of them, such as perennial candytuft and lavender, develop a woody trunk with age, they are called subshrubs. Another group of perennial-type plants has fleshy leaves that can store water for long periods in order to survive drought. These are called succulents and include cacti.

BOTANICAL NOMENCLATURE

The perennials in this book are listed alphabetically by botanical name because some plants have more than one common name. Common names vary according to location, and two plants can sometimes have the same common name.

The first part of a botanical name identifies the specific family—or genus—for example, *Hosta* identifies a large plant family with more than sixty members or species. The second name, such as *Hosta seiboldiana*, identifies a specific wild species that has distinct characteristics, such as large, heart-shaped leaves with a blue luster.

Within a species there can be different varieties. For example *Hosta seiboldiana* 'Frances Williams' identifies a variety with a golden leaf margin. Botanists sometimes differentiate varieties developed in cultivation by calling them cultivars, short for cultivated variety, but the modern tendency is to call them all varieties.

Whenever the symbol " × " appears in a botanical name, it signifies a hybrid— usually the result of crossing different species. For example, *Gaillardia* × *grandiflora* is a cross between *G. arista* and *G. pulchela*, both wild species.

Sometimes flowers are described as single-flowered, meaning they contain a single row of petals (like a daisy). Other flowers are described as double-flowered, which means they have more than one row of petals. Sometimes the doubling is so pronounced and the quantity of petals so many that the flower takes on a globe shape, like a football chrysanthemum.

BENEFITS OF PERENNIALS

The singular advantage of perennials is that you plant them once, and they then flower automatically from year to year. However, this is an oversimplification, since perennials do require care to thrive. Some of the more aggressive kinds will need dividing after several years to stop them from becoming invasive. Also, for a perennial garden to look good, care must be taken that the soil is well fed, taller plants are staked to keep them erect, and plants with a short flowering season are "deadheaded" (the faded flowers are removed) to prevent seed formation and to extend flowering as long as possible.

Perennials add a more sophisticated beauty to gardens than other flowering plant groups. In addition to a great variety of flower forms, they offer a diverse range of growth characteristics (including low and spreading ground-cover effects and vining for tall, vertical accents). Many perennials have exquisite foliage colors, shapes, and textures. Indeed, many, such as ornamental grasses and ferns, are worth growing for their foliage alone.

HOW TO USE PERENNIALS

Perennials are most commonly mixed in beds and borders. The difference between a bed and a border is in the location. A bed is any planting space that is surrounded by grass or some type of paving—in other words, an island of soil, usually round in shape, but often square, rectangular, oval, kidney-shaped, or even triangular. Tall plants are best positioned in the center, and short plants are best planted around the perimeter as an edging.

A border is a strip of soil that usually butts up against some type of backdrop, such as a fence, wall, or hedge. Tall plants are best planted at the rear ("back-of-the-border") and shorter plants sited in front. Beds are usually mounded in the center in order to ensure that drainage is evenly dispersed, and borders generally are higher at the back.

Most perennials require full sun (only a small number will tolerate deep shade), good drainage (although a few will tolerate boggy soil), and regular amounts of water (though a good number are drought-tolerant).

After sunny beds and borders, perennials are most often seen in woodlands and other shady areas, rock gardens, and wetlands (boggy places, ponds, pools, and streams). Perennials can also be components of meadow gardens, cutting gardens, and container gardens.

WOODLANDS AND OTHER SHADY AREAS

It's important to recognize the many kinds of shade. Very few flowering perennials will do well in deep shade. You might improve a shaded location by removing just one overhanging tree limb. If shade comes from a permanent structure, such as a tall building, then it may be possible to brighten the planting spaces with light-reflecting materials, such as white stone gravel or white fencing, or by painting a dark wall white.

Most perennials that will tolerate shade also like a humus-rich soil, particularly one that has been enriched with leaf mold. The soil under trees can often be too shallow for most perennial plants, and so it may be necessary to create island beds around the trunks of trees with an edging of stones, brick, or railroad ties in order to increase the depth of the soil.

ROCK GARDENS

Rock gardens favor the growth of many perennials because a large number of beautiful flowering perennials emanate from alpine environments. The best rock gardens are positioned on sunny slopes. Though water is not absolutely essential, aesthetically these gardens look best when a small stream tumbles down the slope, creating a series of cascades.

Smaller scale rock gardens can be created on dry walls, especially retaining walls, and terrace walls, with plants positioned in cracks so their stems spill over the side of the wall. It is also possible to plant in the crevices of flagstone paths in order to create a small rock garden.

WETLANDS, PONDS, POOLS, AND STREAMS

A few perennials, such as waterlilies, arrowhead, and flag iris, will grow with their roots permanently immersed in water. Others, such as cardinal flowers, lythrum, and swamp mallow, will do better in a permanently moist soil. If a stream runs through your property, the edges are ideal for bog-loving plants, which are best planted in generous drifts. Similarly, if you are fortunate enough to own a natural pond, the margin is ideal for swamp plants. However, since the water level in ponds tends to change over the course of a season, depending on rainfall, you may want to develop some special raised beds around the edge, a little above the normal flood plain, so that plants can be established in good soil without risk of being washed away.

MEADOW GARDENS

A large number of good perennials originate from grassland prairies and are capable of competing with aggressive meadow grasses. These include black-eyed Susans, coneflowers, butterfly weed, and perennial sunflowers. To help establish perennials in a meadow, create islands of bare soil in the meadow and either sow perennial seeds in late summer or establish colonies from young transplants.

Many special wildflower meadow seed mixes combine annuals and perennials, so that the first year some good color is established instantly by the annuals, and the color is continued in years thereafter by the perennials. It is difficult to keep meadow gardens colorful without resorting to native plants. To discover those native plants that might establish themselves permanently in your meadow, tour the area at different times of the year. You may find a particular type of wild penstemon prolific in spring, a rudbeckia colorful in summer, and a wild aster prolific in autumn.

CUTTING GARDENS

Cutting gardens are composed of plants with long stems that last well in water when cut. A large number of perennials are excellent for cutting. The best way to grow them is usually in straight rows like in a vegetable garden, with pathways between each row so plants are easily accessible for cutting. Even if you have a garden large enough for display areas, it's best to reserve a special area for cutting so the flowers for display remain to provide color in the garden. Flowers for cutting are best picked when in a mature bud stage before peak flowering. Since cutting stems before the buds open means they never provide any ornamental garden display, cutting gardens are often conveniently located near a vegetable garden or even combined with vegetables by having flowers and food crops in alternating rows.

CONTAINERS

Though perennials are not as popular as annuals for container gardening—largely because annuals tend to provide a longer floral display—a few perennials do look sensational planted in containers. Most notable are the hardy kinds of hibiscus, dwarf everblooming daylilies (especially 'Stella d'Oro'), and ornamental grasses (such as dwarf pampas plume). The bigger the container, the more suitable it will be for growing perennials. Wood is the preferred container material because it doesn't overheat as easily as plastic or metal. Clay is the next best material, though plants will need more frequent watering because of its porousness.

Good drainage is essential. Though many containers do have drainage holes already drilled in them, these can become clogged unless a piece of wire mesh or a cluster of rough stones is placed over the hole to create air spaces.

The best general-purpose potting soils for perennials are composed of one-third each peat moss, sand, and screened garden topsoil. A slow-release fertilizer should be applied to the soil surface, and watering should be done whenever the soil surface feels dry (usually once a day in summer).

SOIL PREPARATION

Good garden soil is called loam. It has good moisture-holding capacity, yet it allows excessive moisture to drain away freely. It is crumbly, falling apart easily in your hand; is full of air spaces so plant roots can grow through it unhindered; and contains plenty of humus, a spongy material composed of decaying animal and vegetable matter.

Poor garden soil can be sandy at one extreme or clay at the other. Sandy soil cannot hold water, and any plant nutrients are rapidly washed away. However, in other respects, sand is a good growing medium, and when improved by the addition of humus or screened garden topsoil, it can produce excellent plant growth.

Clay soils are lumpy, sticky, cold, and impervious to moisture. Plant roots cannot penetrate them easily. Clay soils direly need aeration, achieved by mixing in large amounts of humus or gypsum.

Humus—the finest soil conditioner for keeping perennial beds healthy—can be added to the soil in the form of garden compost, decayed animal manure, decayed leaves (called leaf mold), and peat moss, sold in large bales at garden centers.

In addition to good soil structure, the chemical balance (or pH content) of the soil must be correct: neither too acid nor too alkaline. Acid soils exist in forested areas with high rainfall; alkaline soils predominate in places where lime deposits are close to the surface and in desert areas. Acid soil can be modified with lime, and alkaline soil with sulphur; to know how much to add, have your soil tested.

When soil is poor, sometimes the gardener's best solution is to build a raised bed above the indigenous soil with landscape ties, brick, or stones and cart in good screened topsoil.

If humus from composted materials is used to condition soil, little or no fertilizer may be necessary for perennials, but many perennials—such as peonies and oriental poppies—are heavy feeders. A slow-release fertilizer raked into the upper soil surface in early spring is generally beneficial.

PROPAGATING PERENNIALS

The easiest way to obtain perennials for your garden is to visit a local nursery and buy them potted up in a ready-to-bloom stage. However, this often requires buying plants in costly, large-capacity containers. Less expensive means of obtaining perennials include mail-order purchase of smaller-size plants and propagation by seed, root division, and cuttings.

Mail-order perennial purchases are generally in small pots or "bare-root" transplants. Garden magazines list numerous mail-order perennial catalogs, including companies that specialize in a particular plant group, such as daylilies or irises. The selection can be much more extensive than that at your local nursery.

Propagation by seed is generally reliable. This is most easily accomplished by sowing the seed into a special nursery bed in late summer, allowing the seedlings to fill out and go dormant over winter, and then transplanting them to permanent locations in early spring for flowering. However, some perennial plants take more than a year to flower; some have seed that requires cold treatment (a period of dormancy at freezing temperatures); or plants may have other idiosyncrasies. Therefore, it is best to read the seed packet carefully to determine the necessary conditions for good germination. Be aware, however, that perennials grown from seed do not always match the parent. Some size and color variation can occur.

By far the easiest way to increase perennial plants is through root division. After a perennial plant has flowered, it starts to increase in size by tillering or offsets, forming a massive root system composed of clumps. By digging up the root mass, you can separate it into smaller clumps, each with a crown of leaves. Each clump will then establish a new colony, identical to the parent in size, color, and growth.

To successfully propagate perennials from cuttings, you need a tray of soil and a heating cable in a protected space, such as a cold frame or greenhouse bench. There are several kinds of cuttings: stem cuttings, leaf cuttings, and root cuttings.

To take stem cuttings, prune off a 3- to 5-inch (7.5 to 13cm) section of a main stem, preferably at the tip of a branch. Dip the cut end into a rooting hormone and insert the cut end into a moist, sandy potting soil. To prevent the soil from drying out too quickly, enclose the rooting tray and the cuttings in a clear plastic bag.

Cuttings need warmth to root, though high heat will inhibit rooting. The best soil temperature is 70°F (21.1°C), plus or minus a few degrees. This is not a problem in summer, but in spring and autumn the use of a heating cable under the tray helps to maintain the 70°F median.

Leaf cuttings are not possible on all perennials but generally succeed with fleshy leaves, such as sedum. You simply snap off a leaf where it attaches to the stem and insert the cut end in potting soil, following the same procedure as for a stem cutting.

Root cuttings are not possible with all perennials, but phlox and oriental poppies are most easily propagated this way. The roots are simply sliced into 2- to 4-inch (5 to 10cm) segments, which are laid horizontally over potting soil and covered with 1 inch (2.5cm) of moist sand. The procedure then is the same as for stem cuttings. Each section of root is capable of sprouting new leaves and roots; pot these up individually until they are large enough to transplant.

The following listing of the most useful perennial plants includes both hardy and tender kinds. They are listed by botanical name, since the common name is not always a reliable means of identification (some perennials may be known by several common names) and common names vary not only from country to country, but within the country itself.

Even the botanical name will change from time to time. For example, *Clematis paniculata* and *Clematis maximowicziana* both describe the same plant, and while taxonomists responsible for classifying plants may favor the use of *maximowicziana* over *paniculata*, it takes some time for nursery growers and seed developers to effect the changes.

CARE OF PERENNIALS

Once the soil has been dug and amended to provide a good planting medium, a few simple gardening chores will ensure good growth and survival of your perennials from year to year.

TRANSPLANTING

Perennial plants purchased from nurseries are mostly offered in pots up to a gallon (4l) capacity. The plant should be removed from its container carefully to keep the root ball intact and to disturb the roots as little as possible. However, if the roots are compacted in the bottom of the pot, it's best to tease them apart and spread them out like an octopus in the bottom of the hole. The root ball should fit snugly in its hole, and the soil should be firmed with the flat of a spade or with feet to ensure good soil contact with the roots. Water each plant thoroughly.

MULCHING

Mulching is the practice of laying a blanket of material—generally organic material—over the soil surface to suffocate weeds. Mulching helps conserve moisture in the soil, and it can also provide protection from winter freezes.

DEADHEADING

Deadheading is the removal of spent flowers to prevent seed formation. It helps the plant conserve energy and produce a longer-lasting floral display.

STAKING

Staking provides the support necessary for many tall-growing perennials such as delphiniums, hollyhocks, and verbascums. Stakes are commonly bamboo with twist-ties to hold stems to the pole. However, the currently preferred "stake" is a wire tower with a flat circular top of wire mesh. The tower is placed over a perennial plant, the flowering stems grow through the mesh, and the plant is self-supporting.

WINTER PROTECTION

Many perennials are sufficiently hardy to survive harsh winters. However, there is a danger from root rot caused by thawing and refreezing. A layer of mulch surrounding perennial plants over winter can help to reduce losses from winterkill.

Some tender perennials can survive harsh winters by being grown in cold frames—the glass lid is closed tight on cold days and opened up on sunny days. Many gardeners in harsh winter climates like to grow delphiniums this way as a means of providing masses of plants from seeds or cuttings. Similarly, pampas plume is too tender for many cold-winter areas but can be overwintered either in a cold frame or in large pots stored in a frost-free place such as a garage or basement.

THE PERENNIALS

ACANTHUS SPINOSUS **(also** ***A. SPINOSISSIMUS)***

COMMON NAME: Bear's-breech

FAMILY: Acanthaceae (Acanthus)

DESCRIPTION: Native to Greece. Displays giant, deeply lobed, shiny, dark green leaves with prominent white veins. Stately clusters of tubular flowers with protruding lower lips are borne on erect spikes. Summer-flowering.

HEIGHT: 2 to 4 feet (.6 to 1.2m).

COLOR: White and purple, white and rose.

HARDINESS: Zones 5 to 9.

CULTURE: Prefers partial shade in hot, dry areas but can be planted in full sun in cooler areas. Requires well-drained, fertile soil. Tolerates drought. Propagate by seed, root division, or stem cuttings in spring.

USES: Ideal for coastal gardens. Makes an excellent accent plant, ground cover. Suitable for fresh and dried arrangements.

ACHILLEA FILIPENDULINA

COMMON NAME: Fern-leaf yarrow

FAMILY: Compositae (Daisies)

DESCRIPTION: Native to Asia. Plants have fernlike green leaves and erect stems bearing 5-inch (12.5cm), flat flower clusters. Late spring- and early summer-flowering.

HEIGHT: 3 feet (.9m).

COLOR: Yellow.

HARDINESS: Zones 4 to 8.

CULTURE: Prefers full sun; tolerates poor soil. Propagated by root division in spring or autumn. Invasive if not divided after two years' growth.

USES: Accent in beds and borders. Cutting, dried arrangements.

ACHILLEA MILLEFOLIUM

COMMON NAME: Common yarrow

FAMILY: Compositae (Daisies)

DESCRIPTION: The variety 'Fire King' is a selection of species native to Europe. Similar to fern-leaf yarrow except for color of flat flower clusters. Late spring- and early summer-flowering.

HEIGHT: 3 feet (.9m).

COLOR: Rosy red.

HARDINESS: Zones 3 to 8.

CULTURE: Prefers full sun; tolerates poor soil. Propagate by root division in spring or autumn. Invasive if not divided after two years' growth.

USES: Accent in beds and borders. Cutting, dried arrangements.

ACHILLEA PTARMICA

COMMON NAME: Sneezewort

FAMILY: Compositae (Daisies)

DESCRIPTION: Native to Europe and Asia. Leaves are narrow, pointed, dark green. The variety 'The Pearl' has double, ¾-inch (2cm), pom-pomlike blooms held erect in loose clusters. Early summer-flowering.

HEIGHT: 2 feet (.6m).

COLOR: White.

HARDINESS: Zones 4 to 9.

CULTURE: Prefers sun. Tolerates poor soil; best in well-drained soil. Propagate by root division in spring or autumn. Invasive if not divided after two years' growth.

USES: Accent in beds and borders (use sparingly). Cutting.

ACONITUM CARMICHAELII (also *A. FISCHERI)*

COMMON NAME: Aconite, monkshood

FAMILY: Ranunculaceae (Buttercups)

DESCRIPTION: Native to Asia. Erect plants have indented, lobed, rich green leaves resembling delphiniums and are topped by clusters of hooded flowers. Late summer-flowering. Caution: All parts are poisonous if ingested.

HEIGHT: 4 feet (1.2m).

COLOR: Blue.

HARDINESS: Zones 3 to 8.

CULTURE: Prefers full sun, moist soil, a cool climate. Grow from seed for blooms the second or third season or propagate by division. Dislikes transplanting.

USES: Tall accent in mixed beds and borders.

ADONIS AMURENSIS

COMMON NAME: Amur adonis, winter adonis

FAMILY: Ranunculaceae (Buttercups)

DESCRIPTION: Native to Siberia. The cup-shaped flowers resemble large winter aconites. Blooms appear on leafless stems in early spring, usually in February or March, and the plant soon produces feathery, deeply indented, green leaves.

HEIGHT: To 18 inches (46cm).

COLOR: Buttercup yellow.

HARDINESS: Zones 4 to 8.

CULTURE: Prefers sun or light shade, well-drained, humus-rich soil. Propagate by division. In rich leaf mold under deciduous trees, plants will reseed and form large colonies.

USES: Massing in rock gardens and woodland gardens.

AEGOPODIUM PODAGRARIA 'VARIEGATUM'

COMMON NAME: Goutweed, bishop's weed

FAMILY: Umbelliferae (Carrots)

DESCRIPTION: Native to Europe. Plants are grown mostly for ivylike, bicolored green-and-white leaves, which form a dense mass. Erect stems topped by 2-inch (5cm) flat flower clusters resembling Queen-Anne's-lace, best removed to prevent self-seeding. Early summer-flowering.

HEIGHT: To 14 inches (36cm).

COLOR: White.

HARDINESS: Zones 4 to 9.

CULTURE: Prefers partial shade but grows in full sun; tolerates poor soil, but prefers well-drained soil. Easily propagated in spring or autumn by root division.

USES: Mostly an edging and deciduous ground cover.

AJUGA REPTANS

COMMON NAME: Carpet bugleweed, blue bugle

FAMILY: Labiatae (Mints)

DESCRIPTION: Native to Europe. Plants form a rosette of oval, pointed, green or bronze leaves and produce spires of tubular flowers. Spring-flowering. The variety 'Burgundy Glow' has green, white, and pink coloring.

HEIGHT: 6 inches (15cm).

COLOR: Blue, white.

HARDINESS: Zones 3 to 8.

CULTURE: Grows in sun or shade; tolerates poor soil, but prefers moist, humus-rich soil. Propagate by seed sown in spring or by division at any time. Can become invasive in lawns.

USES: Edging and flowering ground cover.

ALCHEMILLA VULGARIS
(also *A. MOLLIS*)

COMMON NAME: Lady's-mantle

FAMILY: Rosaceae (Roses)

DESCRIPTION: Native to Europe. Plants form mounds of rounded, scalloped, blue-green leaves and numerous flower clusters. Flowers up to ⅛ inch (3mm) across. Spring-flowering.

HEIGHT: 18 inches (46cm).

COLOR: Yellow.

HARDINESS: Zones 4 to 8.

CULTURE: Prefers full sun or partial shade, moist, humus-rich soil, and good drainage. Propagate by root division.

USES: Ornamental foliage accent for mixed beds and borders. Popular for edging ponds and pools.

AMSONIA TABERNAEMONTANA

COMMON NAME: Bluestar

FAMILY: Apocynaceae (Dogbanes)

DESCRIPTION: Native to Texas. Plants grow erect stems with narrow, pointed, willowlike green leaves and clusters of ½-inch (13mm) star-shaped flowers. Spring-flowering.

HEIGHT: To 3½ feet (1.1m).

COLOR: Blue.

HARDINESS: Zones 4 to 8.

CULTURE: Prefers partial shade. Easy to grow in moist, well-drained loam soil. Propagate by division in spring or autumn.

USES: Accent in mixed beds and borders.

ANAPHALIS TRIPLINERVIS

COMMON NAME: Pearly everlasting

FAMILY: Compositae (Daisies)

DESCRIPTION: Native to the Himalayas. Plants grow erect stems with narrow, pointed, gray-green leaves topped by loose clusters of ½-inch (13mm), papery, buttonlike flowers. Early summer-flowering.

HEIGHT: 12 to 18 inches (31 to 46cm).

COLOR: White.

HARDINESS: Zones 4 to 9.

CULTURE: Prefers full sun but tolerates light shade. Needs well-drained moist soil. Propagate by root division in spring or autumn.

USES: Accent in beds and borders. Popular for cutting and dried arrangements. Popular component of all-white gardens.

ANCHUSA AZUREA (also *A. ITALICA*)

COMMON NAME: Bugloss, Italian bugloss

FAMILY: Boraginaceae (Borages)

DESCRIPTION: Native to the Mediterranean region. Plants grow large, smooth, spear-shaped leaves, erect stems, and immense clusters of ½-inch (13mm) flowers; resembles a giant forget-me-not. Spring-flowering.

HEIGHT: 4 to 5 feet (1.2 to 1.5m).

COLOR: Bright blue.

HARDINESS: Zones 4 to 8.

CULTURE: Easily grown in full sun or light shade. Needs well-drained soil. Propagated by seed direct-sown in spring or by division in spring or autumn.

USES: Tall accent in mixed beds and borders. A dwarf variety, 'Little John', is used for massing and edging.

ANEMONE × HYBRIDA (also *A. JAPONICA*)

COMMON NAME: Japanese anemone

FAMILY: Ranunculaceae (Buttercups)

DESCRIPTION: Native to Japan. Plants grow clumps of trifoliate, toothed dark green leaves from which emerge tall, slender stems topped with 3-inch (7.5cm) single or double flowers. Late summer- or early autumn-flowering.

HEIGHT: 4 to 5 feet (1.2 to 1.5m).

COLOR: Pink, white.

HARDINESS: Zones 6 to 8.

CULTURE: Prefers sun but tolerates light shade. Needs humus-rich, well-drained soil. In cold climates, mulching can protect from severe freezing. Propagate by division in spring.

USES: Tall accent in mixed beds and borders.

ANEMONE NEMOROSA

COMMON NAME: European wood anemone

FAMILY: Ranunculaceae (Buttercups)

DESCRIPTION: Native to Europe. Low, clump-forming plants grow in colonies that spread by underground rhizomes. Green leaves are toothed and heavily indented; flowers are star-shaped, ½ to ¾ inches (13 to 19mm) long. Spring-flowering.

HEIGHT: To 8 inches (20cm).

COLOR: White, pale pink.

HARDINESS: Zones 4 to 8.

CULTURE: Prefers light shade; humus-rich, well-drained loam soil. Propagate by seed direct-sown or by division.

USES: Effective massed as an edging to shady beds and borders; also woodland wildflower gardens.

ANEMONE SYLVESTRIS

COMMON NAME: Snowdrop anemone

FAMILY: Ranunculaceae (Buttercups)

DESCRIPTION: Native to Europe. Plants have five-fingered, toothed green leaves. Slender stems hold 2-inch (5cm), cup-shaped flowers well above the foliage. Spring-flowering.

HEIGHT: To 18 inches (46cm).

COLOR: White.

HARDINESS: Zones 4 to 9.

CULTURE: Prefers light shade, moist, humus-rich soil. Propagate by seed and by division.

USES: Best in woodland wildflower gardens, massed around the trunks of trees, and along rustic paths.

ANIGOZANTHOS FLAVIDUS

COMMON NAME: Kangaroo-paw

FAMILY: Haemodoraceae (Bloodworts)

DESCRIPTION: Native to Australia. Plants grow slender, green, grasslike leaves and erect, woolly stems topped by tubular flowers clustered to resemble the paws of a kangaroo. Flowers are up to 1¼ inches (3cm) long. Summer-flowering.

HEIGHT: 3 to 4 feet (.9 to 1.2m).

COLOR: Red.

HARDINESS: Zones 9 to 10.

CULTURE: Easy to grow in full sun; tolerates drought. Likes well-drained, leafy, acid soil. Propagate by root division in spring.

USES: Good accent in mixed beds and borders. Combines well with ornamental grasses.

ANTHEMIS SANCTI-JOHANNIS

COMMON NAME: Dog fennel, St. John's chamomile

FAMILY: Compositae (Daisies)

DESCRIPTION: Native to Bulgaria. Plants grow clumps of fernlike, aromatic green leaves and numerous erect stems topped by 2-inch (5cm), daisylike flowers. Summer-flowering.

HEIGHT: 2 to 3 feet (.6 to .9m).

COLOR: Yellow-orange.

HARDINESS: Zones 4 to 8.

CULTURE: Prefers full sun, good drainage. Propagate mostly by root division in spring or autumn.

USES: Massed in mixed beds and borders. Good for cutting.

ANTHEMIS TINCTORIA

COMMON NAME: Golden marguerite

FAMILY: Compositae (Daisies)

DESCRIPTION: Native to the Mediterranean region. Billowing, bushy plants grow fernlike green leaves and masses of 2-inch (5cm), daisylike flowers. Early summer-flowering.

HEIGHT: 3 feet (.9m).

COLOR: Yellow.

HARDINESS: Zones 4 to 8.

CULTURE: Prefers full sun; tolerates heat and drought. Prefers well-drained soil. Propagate by root division in spring or autumn. Aggressive plants may need dividing every year.

USES: Massed in beds and borders; container plantings. Suitable for cutting.

AQUILEGIA ALPINA

COMMON NAME: Alpine columbine

FAMILY: Ranunculaceae (Buttercups)

DESCRIPTION: Several popular garden varieties in mixed colors have been developed in the United States from the wild species native to the Rocky mountains. Light, airy, delicate appearance. Feathery, gray-green leaves and slender stems are topped by nodding, 2½-inch (6.5cm), star-shaped flowers with long spurs and curiously folded inner petals. The whole floral structure resembles a granny's bonnet. Spring-flowering.

HEIGHT: 1 to 2 feet (.3 to .6m).

COLOR: Clear blue.

HARDINESS: Zones 4 to 7.

CULTURE: Plants prefer full sun, fertile soil, excellent drainage. Sow seed 10 weeks before autumn frosts, or propagate by root division.

USES: Massed in beds and borders. Good cut flower.

ARABIS CAUCASICA

COMMON NAME: Wall rock cress

FAMILY: Cruciferae (Mustards)

DESCRIPTION: Native to the Caucasus mountains of Europe. Low, spreading plants form rosettes of wrinkled, tonguelike green leaves and loose clusters of small, four-petaled flowers ⅜ to ⅝ inches (9 to 16mm) long. Spring- and early summer-flowering.

HEIGHT: 12 inches (31cm).

COLOR: White, pink.

HARDINESS: Zones 4 to 8.

CULTURE: Prefers full sun but tolerates light shade; needs good drainage. Propagate by root division in spring or autumn.

USES: Rock gardens, dry walls; edging beds and borders.

ARCTOTHECA CALENDULA

COMMON NAME: Cape-weed

FAMILY: Compositae (Daisies)

DESCRIPTION: Native to South Africa. Plants form rosettes of heavily indented, gray-green leaves that tolerate crowding and create a weed-suffocating ground cover. Slender stems are topped with 2-inch (5cm), daisylike flowers. Summer-flowering.

HEIGHT: 12 inches (31cm).

COLOR: Yellow.

HARDINESS: Zones 9 to 10.

CULTURE: Prefers full sun, well-drained, fertile soil. Likes a coastal, relatively frost-free climate. Propagate by seed; plants self-seed readily.

USES: Mostly used as a ground cover. Especially popular in Mediterranean-type climates to decorate slopes and control erosion.

ARENARIA VERNA

COMMON NAME: Sandwort, Irish moss

FAMILY: Caryophyllaceae (Pinks)

DESCRIPTION: Native to Europe. Low-growing turflike plants resemble mounds of moss. Leaves are small, narrow, and dark green, and tiny, daisylike flowers cover the plants like a pincushion. Spring-flowering. The variety 'Aurea' has yellow-green foliage.

HEIGHT: 2 inches (5cm).

COLOR: White.

HARDINESS: Zones 5 to 8.

CULTURE: Prefers full sun and almost daily watering in well-drained sandy or loam soil. Best to propagate by division.

USES: Edging beds and borders; cracks in flagstone. Suitable for coastal gardens.

ARMERIA MARITIMA

COMMON NAME: Thrift, sea pink

FAMILY: Plumbaginaceae (Plumbagos)

DESCRIPTION: Native to the coasts of Europe. Plants form low, spreading, mounded clumps of grasslike, blue-green leaves and slender stalks topped by 1-inch (2.5cm) rounded clusters of tiny florets. Summer-flowering.

HEIGHT: 10 inches (25cm).

COLOR: Mostly pink.

HARDINESS: Zones 4 to 7.

CULTURE: Prefers full sun, good drainage; tolerates sandy soil, salt spray, high winds. Propagate by root division in spring or autumn.

USES: Massed in beds and borders; dry walls, rock gardens; edging.

ARTEMISIA LUDOVICIANA ALBULA

COMMON NAME: Silver-king artemisia

FAMILY: Compositae (Daisies)

DESCRIPTION: Native to the midwestern and western United States. Bushy, erect plants grow slender, pointed, silvery leaves. Inconspicuous flowers are borne in clusters at ends of the leafy stems. Late summer- and autumn-flowering.

HEIGHT: 3 feet (.9m).

COLOR: White.

HARDINESS: Zones 5 to 8.

CULTURE: Prefers full sun, good drainage; tolerates poor soil, heat, drought. Propagate by root division in spring or autumn.

USES: Accent in mixed beds and borders. Popular for creating herbal wreaths.

ARUNCUS DIOICUS

COMMON NAME: Goatsbeard

FAMILY: Rosaceae (Roses)

DESCRIPTION: Native to the northwest coast of North America. Plants form a bushy clump of oval, pointed, heavily veined green leaves arranged in threes. Erect stalks support wispy flower plumes that can measure up to 10 inches (25cm). Male and female flowers grow on separate plants. Spring-flowering.

HEIGHT: 5 feet (1.5m).

COLOR: White.

HARDINESS: Zones 4 to 9.

CULTURE: Prefers light shade but will take full sun and moist soil. Propagate by root division in spring or autumn.

USES: Dominant accent in mixed beds and borders. Good massed along stream banks and pond margins.

ASCLEPIAS TUBEROSA

COMMON NAME: Butterfly weed

FAMILY: Asclepiadaceae (Milkweeds)

DESCRIPTION: Native to the north-eastern United States. Erect stems with oval leaves are topped by dense, flat clusters of star-shaped flowers that attract butterflies. Late spring-flowering.

HEIGHT: 3 feet (1.5m).

COLOR: Orange, yellow, red.

HARDINESS: Zones 4 to 9.

CULTURE: Prefers full sun and hot summers; tolerates sandy soil, competition from meadow grasses. Likes humus-rich, well-drained soil. Propagate by seed or by division in spring or autumn.

USES: Accent in mixed beds and borders, rock gardens, wildflower meadows. Excellent cut flower.

ASPHODELINE LUTEA

COMMON NAME: Asphodel, king's-spear

FAMILY: Liliaceae (Lilies)

DESCRIPTION: Native to the Mediterranean region. Slender, grasslike gray-green leaves surround a stiff stalk with a spike of fragrant, 1-inch (2.5cm), star-shaped flowers. Early summer-flowering.

HEIGHT: 3 feet (1.5m).

COLOR: Yellow.

HARDINESS: Zones 6 to 9.

CULTURE: Prefers full sun, well-drained soil; tolerates light shade. Propagate by root division in spring or autumn.

USES: Tall accent in mixed beds and borders. Good for cutting.

ASTER ALPINUS

COMMON NAME: Michaelmas daisy, Alpine aster

FAMILY: Compositae (Daisies)

DESCRIPTION: Native to mountains of Europe and Asia. Compact, rosette-forming plants have lancelike, green leaves and 2-inch (5cm) daisylike flowers. Spring-flowering, with continuous intermittent bloom.

HEIGHT: To 9 inches (23cm).

COLOR: Blue to violet with yellow button center.

HARDINESS: Zones 5 to 7.

CULTURE: Prefers full sun, well-drained sandy or loam soil. Best to propagate by division, but also possible by seed.

USES: Rock gardens; edging beds and borders; cracks in flagstone.

ASTER × FRIKARTII

COMMON NAME: Michaelmas daisy

FAMILY: Compositae (Daisies)

DESCRIPTION: Developed from species native to Europe and North America. Plants grow clumps of lancelike leaves and erect stems that branch heavily at the top and are covered with lightly fragrant, 2- to 3-inch (5 to 7.5cm), daisylike flowers. Summer-flowering.

HEIGHT: 3 feet (.9m).

COLOR: Lavender-blue with yellow center.

HARDINESS: Zones 5 to 9.

CULTURE: Prefers full sun, good drainage. Mulching helps prevent winterkill in cold-winter areas. Propagate by root division.

USES: Beautiful accent in mixed beds and borders. Exquisite cut flower.

ASTER NOVAE-ANGLIAE

COMMON NAME: New England aster

FAMILY: Compositae (Daisies)

DESCRIPTION: Native to New England and other northeastern areas of the United States. Plants form vigorous clumps of erect stems with narrow, pointed green leaves and masses of 1½-inch (4cm), daisylike flowers. Autumn-flowering.

HEIGHT: 4 to 5 feet (1.2 to 1.5m).

COLOR: Includes lavender-blue, white, red, pink.

HARDINESS: Zones 5 to 8.

CULTURE: Prefers full sun, good drainage. Propagate by root division in spring or autumn and by seed in spring or summer. May need staking to keep the top-heavy flower stems erect.

USES: Good accent in mixed beds and borders. Excellent cut flower.

ASTER NOVI-BELGII HYBRIDS

COMMON NAME: Michaelmas daisy, New York aster

FAMILY: Compositae (Daisies)

DESCRIPTION: Developed from crosses with European asters, particularly *A. dumosus*. Plants are mostly low-growing and mound-shaped with lancelike, toothed, green leaves and masses of 1-inch (2.5cm), daisylike flowers. Late summer- and early autumn-flowering.

HEIGHT: 1 to 2 feet (.3 to .6m).

COLOR: Mostly blue, red shades.

HARDINESS: Zones 4 to 8.

CULTURE: Prefers full sun, well-drained sandy or loam soil. Best to propagate by division.

USES: Massing in beds and borders.

ASTER TATARICUS

COMMON NAME: Tartarian aster

FAMILY: Compositae (Daisies)

DESCRIPTION: Native to Siberia. Plants grow vigorous clumps of erect stems with broad, pointed, lustrous green leaves and large clusters of 1-inch (2.5cm), daisylike flowers. Late summer-flowering.

HEIGHT: 6 feet (1.8m).

COLOR: Purple.

HARDINESS: Zones 4 to 8.

CULTURE: Prefers full sun; tolerates moist and dry soil but prefers fertile soil. Propagate by division. May need staking to support heavy flower clusters.

USES: Tall accent in mixed beds and borders. Effective planted along stream margins and around large ponds.

ASTILBE × ARENDSII

COMMON NAME: Spiraea

FAMILY: Saxifragaceae (Saxifrages)

DESCRIPTION: Developed from species native to China. Plants form a dense mound of finely cut green leaves and airy stems with handsome flower spikes composed of numerous tiny flowers. Early summer-flowering.

HEIGHT: 3 to 4 feet (.9 to 1.2m).

COLOR: Mostly white, pink, red.

HARDINESS: Zones 5 to 8.

CULTURE: Grows in sun or light shade; prefers moist, fertile soil. Propagate by root division in spring or autumn.

USES: Massing along stream banks and pond margins; good accent in beds and borders.

ASTILBE CHINENSIS

COMMON NAME: Spiraea, Chinese astilbe

FAMILY: Saxifragaceae (Saxifrages)

DESCRIPTION: Native to China. Plants are perfect miniatures of standard astilbes, growing clumps of feathery, dark green leaves and erect stems topped with tapering flower spikes. Early summer-flowering.

HEIGHT: 12 inches (31 cm).

COLOR: Soft pink.

HARDINESS: Zones 5 to 8.

CULTURE: Grows in sun or light shade; tolerates both moist and dry soils but prefers fertile soil. Propagate by division.

USES: Excellent for edging beds and borders. Good accent in rock gardens and for decorating the edges of small ponds and pools.

AUBRIETA DELTOIDEA

COMMON NAME: Rockcress

FAMILY: Cruciferae (Mustards)

DESCRIPTION: Native to Europe. Low-growing, compact plants produce oval, pointed green leaves and masses of ½-inch (13mm), four-petaled flowers. Spring-flowering.

HEIGHT: 6 inches (15cm).

COLOR: Mostly purple.

HARDINESS: Zones 5 to 7.

CULTURE: Prefers full sun, good drainage, and cool weather. Propagate by root division or seed.

USES: Edging beds and borders; rock gardens; mixed container plantings incorporating flowering bulbs.

AURINIA SAXATILIS

COMMON NAME: Basket-of-gold

FAMILY: Cruciferae (Mustards)

DESCRIPTION: Native to Europe. Low-growing, spreading plants form a dense mat of spear-shaped, gray-green leaves and masses of small, four-petaled flowers. Spring-flowering.

HEIGHT: 6 to 12 inches (15 to 31cm).

COLOR: Mostly golden yellow, lemon yellow.

HARDINESS: Zones 4 to 7.

CULTURE: Plants prefer full sun, excellent drainage, poor soil. Start seed in spring or summer for flowering the following season.

USES: Low accent in mixed beds and borders, especially those featuring tulips. Also good for dry walls and rock gardens.

BAPTISIA AUSTRALIS

COMMON NAME: Blue false indigo

FAMILY: Leguminosae (Peas)

DESCRIPTION: Native to the southern United States, especially Texas. Bushy plants grow cloverlike bright green leaves and lupinelike flower spikes. Individual flowers are up to 1 inch (2.5cm) long. Spring-flowering, then develops black beanlike seed pods.

HEIGHT: 4 feet (1.2m).

COLOR: Blue.

HARDINESS: Zones 4 to 9.

CULTURE: Prefers full sun, excellent drainage; tolerates sandy and stony soil. Propagate by seed or root division.

USES: Accent in mixed beds and borders; rock gardens.

BEGONIA GRANDIS

COMMON NAME: Hardy begonia

FAMILY: Begoniaceae (Begonias)

DESCRIPTION: Native to China and Japan. Plants produce a billowing clump of heart-shaped, serrated leaves and sparse flower clusters with 1-inch (2.5cm), begonia-like flowers on red stems. Late summer-flowering.

HEIGHT: 2½ feet (.8m).

COLOR: Pink.

HARDINESS: Zone 7 south (zone 6 with mulch protection and sheltered position).

CULTURE: Prefers light shade, moist, humus-rich soil, good drainage. Propagate from cuttings but also from bulbils that grow in the leaf joints and drop to the ground like seeds.

USES: Massed in beds and borders.

BERGENIA CORDIFOLIA

COMMON NAME: Heartleaf

FAMILY: Saxifragaceae (Saxifrages)

DESCRIPTION: Native to Siberia. Plants form rosettes of shiny, green or bronze leaves with slender stalks topped by loose clusters of ½-inch (13mm) flowers. Early spring-flowering.

HEIGHT: 18 inches (46cm).

COLOR: Mostly pink, red, purple, white.

HARDINESS: Zones 3 to 8.

CULTURE: Prefers light shade, moist, humus-rich soil. Propagate by root division.

USES: Mostly a ground cover, especially along stream banks and pond margins. Beautiful in woodland gardens.

BOLTONIA ASTEROIDES

COMMON NAME: White boltonia

FAMILY: Compositae (Daisies)

DESCRIPTION: Native to North America. Plants grow narrow, pointed leaves and upright stems with a cloud of 1-inch (2.5cm), daisylike flowers; resemble Michaelmas daisies. Late summer- and early autumn-flowering.

HEIGHT: 5 feet (1.5m).

COLOR: White, pale pink.

HARDINESS: Zone 4 south.

CULTURE: Prefers full sun, moist, fertile soil, good drainage. Propagate by root division in spring or autumn. May need staking to keep the top-heavy flower stems erect.

USES: Tall accent in mixed beds and borders. Suitable for cutting. Combines well with ornamental grasses, such as *Miscanthus* species.

BRUNNERA MACROPHYLLA

COMMON NAME: Siberian bugloss

FAMILY: Boraginaceae (Borages)

DESCRIPTION: Native to Siberia. Plants grow clumps of heart-shaped, dark green leaves and clusters of ¼-inch (6mm), star-shaped flowers; resemble forget-me-nots. Spring-flowering.

HEIGHT: 18 inches (46cm).

COLOR: Light blue.

HARDINESS: Zones 4 to 8.

CULTURE: Prefers light shade and moist, humus-rich soil though tolerates poor soil. Propagate by root division.

USES: Edging beds and borders. Especially attractive along paths in woodland gardens.

CALTHA PALUSTRIS

COMMON NAME: Marsh marigold

FAMILY: Ranunculaceae (Buttercups)

DESCRIPTION: Native to Europe. Plants grow clumps of shiny, heart-shaped, green leaves and loose clusters of 2-inch (5cm) flowers resembling buttercups. The variety 'Flore Pleno' has globular double flowers. Early spring-flowering.

HEIGHT: 2 feet (.6m).

COLOR: Yellow.

HARDINESS: Zones 4 to 9.

CULTURE: Grows in sun or light shade; prefers a moist, rich soil; will grow even in boggy soil. Propagate by root division or seed.

USES: Mostly along the boggy margins of streams and ponds.

CAMPANULA CARPATICA

COMMON NAME: Tussock bellflower, Carpathian harebell

FAMILY: Campanulaceae (Bellflowers)

DESCRIPTION: Native to eastern Europe. Plants grow clumps of small, spear-shaped green leaves and erect stems with 2-inch (5cm), bell-shaped flowers. Spring- or autumn-flowering when nights are cool.

HEIGHT: 12 inches (31cm).

COLOR: Blue.

HARDINESS: Zones 4 to 7.

CULTURE: Prefers full sun and moist, fertile, well-drained soil. Propagate by seed and division.

USES: Edging beds and borders; rock gardens, cracks in flagstone.

CAMPANULA GLOMERATA

COMMON NAME: Clustered bellflower

FAMILY: Campanulaceae (Bellflowers)

DESCRIPTION: Native to Europe. Plants form clumps of erect stems with heart-shaped green leaves topped with 3-inch (7.5cm), globular clusters of bell-shaped flowers. Early summer-blooming.

HEIGHT: 3 feet (.9m).

COLOR: Blue, white.

HARDINESS: Zones 3 to 8.

CULTURE: Prefers full sun; tolerates moist soil but prefers fertile, well-drained soil. Propagate by root division in spring or autumn.

USES: Accent in mixed beds and borders. Good for cutting.

CAMPANULA LATIFOLIA

COMMON NAME: Great bellflower

FAMILY: Campanulaceae (Bellflowers)

DESCRIPTION: Native to Europe. Plants grow heart-shaped, dark green leaves and clusters of erect stems studded at the top with cup-shaped flowers up to 3 inches (7.5cm) across. Late spring- and early summer-flowering.

HEIGHT: 3 to 4 feet (.9 to 1.2 m).

COLOR: Blue.

HARDINESS: Zones 4 to 8.

CULTURE: Prefers full sun but tolerates light shade. Likes fertile, well-drained soil. Propagate by seed and root division. May need staking.

USES: Accent in mixed beds and borders. Good for cutting.

CAMPANULA PERSICIFOLIA

COMMON NAME: Willow bellflower, peach-bells

FAMILY: Campanulaceae (Bellflowers)

DESCRIPTION: Native to Europe. Plants grow clumps of erect stems with slender, pointed green leaves, topped by flower spikes of star-shaped flowers. Individual flowers are 1½ inches (4cm). Early summer-blooming.

HEIGHT: 3 feet (.9m).

COLOR: Blue, white.

HARDINESS: Zones 4 to 8.

CULTURE: Prefers full sun and moist, fertile soil. Will repeat-bloom in late summer if faded flower stems are removed. May need staking.

USES: Tall accent in mixed beds and borders.

CAMPANULA PORTENSCHLAGIANA

COMMON NAME: Creeping bellflower, dalmatian bellflower

FAMILY: Campanulaceae (Bellflowers)

DESCRIPTION: Native to Europe. Low, spreading plants form mounds of small, oval green leaves and masses of 1-inch (2.5cm), star-shaped flowers. Spring-flowering.

HEIGHT: To 8 inches (20cm).

COLOR: Blue.

HARDINESS: Zones 4 to 7.

CULTURE: Prefers full sun, well-drained, gritty, sandy or loam soil. Propagate by seed and division.

USES: Mostly a ground cover in rock gardens; edging beds and borders; cascading down dry walls.

CAMPANULA POSCHARSKYANA

COMMON NAME: Dwarf bellflower, Serbian bellflower

FAMILY: Campanulaceae (Bellflowers)

DESCRIPTION: Native to Europe. Plants form spreading clumps of serrated, pointed green leaves and masses of 1-inch (2.5cm), star-shaped flowers. Spring-flowering; best during cool conditions.

HEIGHT: 6 inches (15cm).

COLOR: Blue.

HARDINESS: Zones 4 to 7.

CULTURE: Prefers full sun, excellent drainage; tolerates drought. Propagate by seed and root division.

USES: Rock gardens, dry walls; suitable for cracks in flagstone.

CARPOBROTUS EDULIS

COMMON NAME: Hottentot fig

FAMILY: Aizoaceae (Carpetweeds)

DESCRIPTION: Native to South Africa. Plants form a dense carpet of angular, succulent leaves and shimmering, 4-inch (10cm), daisylike flowers. Leaves are multicolored—usually green, but also orange, red, and bronze. Spring-flowering, then forms a figlike fruit.

HEIGHT: 4 to 6 inches (10 to 15cm).

COLOR: Yellow, purple, pink.

HARDINESS: Zones 9 to 10.

CULTURE: Prefers a seashore exposure and full sun; requires excellent drainage; tolerates sandy soil—even pure sand—and drought. Propagate by root division.

USES: Ground cover to control soil erosion.

CATANANCHE CAERULEA

COMMON NAME: Cupid's-dart

FAMILY: Compositae (Daisies)

DESCRIPTION: Native to southern Europe. Plants grow slender, pointed, grasslike, gray-green leaves and wiry stems topped with 2-inch (5cm) cornflowerlike flowers. Summer-flowering.

HEIGHT: 2 to 3 feet (.6 to .9m).

COLOR: Pale blue.

HARDINESS: Zones 5 to 8.

CULTURE: Prefers full sun; tolerates poor soil, heat, drought. Best to propagate by seed and root division. Will flower first year from seed started early indoors and direct-sown.

USES: Mixed beds and borders. Cutting, dried arrangements.

CENTAUREA HYPOLEUCA

COMMON NAME: Knapweed, perennial cornflower

FAMILY: Compositae (Daisies)

DESCRIPTION: Native to Turkey. Plants grow bushy mounds of heavily serrated leaves, which are green on top, whitish underneath; and 2-inch (5cm) cornflowerlike flowers. Summer-blooming.

HEIGHT: 2 feet (.6m).

COLOR: Pale blue.

HARDINESS: Zones 4 to 8.

CULTURE: Prefers full sun, well-drained, fertile soil. Propagate by division.

USES: Mixed beds and borders. Good for cutting.

CENTAUREA MACROCEPHALA

COMMON NAME: Knapweed, globe centaurea

FAMILY: Compositae (Daisies)

DESCRIPTION: Native to Armenia. Plants grow vigorous clumps of broad, straplike, pointed green leaves and strong stems topped with 3½-inch (9cm) flowers resembling shaving brushes. Early summer-blooming.

HEIGHT: 3 feet (.9m).

COLOR: Yellow.

HARDINESS: Zones 3 to 8.

CULTURE: Prefers full sun, good drainage. Will grow in poor soil. Propagate by division.

USES: Accent in mixed beds and borders. Popular for drying.

CENTAUREA MONTANA

COMMON NAME: Mountain bluet

FAMILY: Compositae (Daisies)

DESCRIPTION: Native to central Europe. Plants form mounded clumps of serrated green leaves and slender stems topped by 3-inch (7.5cm), cornflowerlike flowers. Early summer-flowering.

HEIGHT: 2 feet (.6m).

COLOR: Blue.

HARDINESS: Zones 3 to 8.

CULTURE: Prefers full sun, good drainage. Will grow in poor soil. Best to propagate by division.

USES: Accent for mixed beds and borders. Good for cutting.

CENTRANTHUS RUBER

COMMON NAME: Red valerian

FAMILY: Valerianaceae (Valerians)

DESCRIPTION: Native to the Mediterranean region. Plants form erect clumps of spear-shaped, green leaves and slender stems topped by dense clusters of small flowers. Individual flowers are approximately ½ inch (13mm) long. Late spring- and autumn-flowering; best during cool weather.

HEIGHT: 2 to 3 feet (.6 to .9m).

COLOR: Red, white.

HARDINESS: Zones 5 to 9.

CULTURE: Prefers full sun, good drainage. Thrives in poor, alkaline soil. Propagate by seed and root division.

USES: Mixed beds and borders; rock gardens, dry walls.

CERASTIUM TOMENTOSUM

COMMON NAME: Snow-in-summer

FAMILY: Caryophyllaceae (Pinks)

DESCRIPTION: Native to Europe. Low-growing, spreading plants form a carpet of small, narrow, woolly, silvery leaves covered with myriads of 1-inch (2.5cm), star-shaped flowers that are dazzling on a sunny day. Spring-flowering.

HEIGHT: 6 to 8 inches (15 to 20cm).

COLOR: White.

HARDINESS: Zones 4 to 7.

CULTURE: Prefers full sun, excellent drainage, dry soil. Best to propagate by division.

USES: Mostly edging beds and borders and as drifts in rock gardens and dry walls. Good ground cover for sandy soils.

CERATOSTIGMA PLUMBAGINOIDES

COMMON NAME: Leadwort

FAMILY: Plumbaginaceae (Plumbagos)

DESCRIPTION: Native to China. Low-growing plants form dense, spreading mats of tonguelike, fleshy, green leaves and small terminal clusters of 1-inch (2.5cm) flowers. Late summer-flowering.

HEIGHT: 12 inches (31cm).

COLOR: Deep blue.

HARDINESS: Zones 5 to 8.

CULTURE: Prefers full sun but tolerates light shade; requires good drainage and good soil. Best to propagate by division.

USES: Mostly edging beds and borders; also as drifts in rock gardens.

CHRYSANTHEMUM FRUTESCENS

COMMON NAME: Marguerite

FAMILY: Compositae (Daisies)

DESCRIPTION: Native to the Canary Islands. Plants form mounds of indented green leaves and masses of 2-inch (5cm), daisylike flowers. Spring-flowering.

HEIGHT: 2 to 3 feet (.6 to .9m).

COLOR: White, yellow, pink.

HARDINESS: Zones 9 to 10. A tender perennial for mild-winter climates, such as the Mediterranean; grown as a greenhouse pot plant in areas with cold winters.

CULTURE: Prefers full sun, good drainage. Propagate by seed and division. Cutting back stems after flowers are faded will promote repeat blooms.

USES: Mixed beds and borders; containers.

CHRYSANTHEMUM LEUCANTHEMUM

COMMON NAME: Oxeye daisy

FAMILY: Compositae (Daisies)

DESCRIPTION: Native to Europe; naturalized throughout North America. Plants grow clumps of toothed green leaves and erect, slender stems topped by 1½- to 2-inch (4 to 5cm) daisies. Late spring-flowering.

HEIGHT: 2 feet (.6m).

COLOR: White with bright yellow center.

HARDINESS: Zone 3.

CULTURE: Prefers full sun, good drainage, reasonably fertile soil. Propagate by seed or division.

USES: Mixed beds and borders. Popular component of wildflower meadow mixtures. Excellent for cutting.

CHRYSANTHEMUM × *MORIFOLIUM*

COMMON NAME: Florist's chrysanthemum, cushion mum, football mum

FAMILY: Compositae (Daisies)

DESCRIPTION: Hybridized from species native to China. Plants differ in habit according to variety. Some form mounds with star-shaped or pom-pom blooms (called cushion mums), and others are tall-growing with double globular blooms (called football mums). Leaves are green, indented. Autumn-flowering.

HEIGHT: 1 to 3 feet (.3 to .9m).

COLOR: Red, yellow, pink, orange, purple, bronze, white.

HARDINESS: Depends on variety; usually grown for one season's bloom.

CULTURE: Prefers full sun, well-drained, humus-rich loam soil. Best to propagate by stem cuttings taken in autumn and raised under glass. Cushion mums need pinching to keep them compact; tall kinds may need staking.

USES: Cushion mums are massed in beds and borders; taller kinds are excellent for cutting.

CHRYSANTHEMUM × *SUPERBUM*

COMMON NAME: Shasta daisy

FAMILY: Compositae (Daisies)

DESCRIPTION: Hybridized from species native to Europe and Asia. Plants grow slender, serrated green leaves and erect stems topped by 2- to 4-inch (5 to 10cm) daisylike flowers. Midsummer-flowering.

HEIGHT: 1 to 2½ feet (.3 to .8m).

COLOR: White.

HARDINESS: Zones 4 to 8.

CULTURE: Prefers full sun, fertile loam soil. Best to propagate by root division. Some dwarf kinds will flower the first year from seed started early indoors.

USES: Accent in mixed beds and borders. Excellent for cutting.

CHRYSOGONUM VIRGINIANUM

COMMON NAME: Golden star

FAMILY: Compositae (Daisies)

DESCRIPTION: Native to the northeastern and southern United States. Low-growing, spreading plants have lancelike dark green leaves and masses of 1½-inch (4cm), star-shaped flowers. Spring-flowering.

HEIGHT: 4 to 6 inches (10 to 15cm).

COLOR: Golden yellow.

HARDINESS: Zones 5 to 8.

CULTURE: Grows in sun or light shade; needs peaty, sandy soil and good drainage. Best to propagate by seed and root division.

USES: Ground cover; edging beds and borders.

CHRYSOPSIS VILLOSA

COMMON NAME: Golden aster

FAMILY: Compositae (Daisies)

DESCRIPTION: Native to the eastern United States. Plants grow narrow green leaves, erect stems, and dense clusters of 1½-inch (4cm) asterlike flowers. Late summer-flowering.

HEIGHT: 4 to 5 feet (1.2 to 1.5m).

COLOR: Golden yellow.

HARDINESS: Zones 5 to 8.

CULTURE: Grows in sun or light shade; tolerates dry, sandy soil. Needs good drainage. Best to propagate by division.

USES: Tall accent in mixed beds and borders.

CIMICIFUGA RACEMOSA

COMMON NAME: Black cohosh, black snakeroot

FAMILY: Ranunculaceae (Buttercups)

DESCRIPTION: Native to the eastern United States. Plants grow clumps of compound green leaves composed of small leaflets and erect stems topped by 1- to 1½-foot (.3 to .5m) flower spikes. Midsummer-flowering.

HEIGHT: 6 feet (1.8m).

COLOR: White.

HARDINESS: Zones 3 to 8.

CULTURE: Grows in sun or light shade. Prefers moist, humus-rich soil. Needs good drainage. Best to propagate by root division.

USES: Tall background in beds and borders; woodland wildflower gardens. Good for cutting.

COREOPSIS LANCEOLATA

COMMON NAME: Tickseed, lance-leaf coreopsis

FAMILY: Compositae (Daisies)

DESCRIPTION: Native to the south-eastern United States. Plants grow bushy clumps of slender, pointed, lancelike dark green leaves and erect stems topped with 2½-inch (6.5cm), daisylike flowers. Early summer-flowering.

HEIGHT: 3 feet (.9m).

COLOR: Yellow.

HARDINESS: Zones 4 to 9.

CULTURE: Prefers full sun; tolerates dry, sandy soil. Needs good drainage. Best to propagate by division. Some dwarf kinds will flower the first year from seed started early indoors.

USES: Highlight in mixed beds and borders; a popular component of wild-flower meadows.

COREOPSIS ROSEA

COMMON NAME: Tickseed, pink coreopsis

FAMILY: Compositae (Daisies)

DESCRIPTION: Native to Mexico. Plants form mounded clumps of narrow, pointed green leaves and masses of ¾-inch (19mm) daisylike flowers. Early summer-flowering.

HEIGHT: 12 inches (31cm).

COLOR: Pink.

HARDINESS: Zones 4 to 9.

CULTURE: Prefers full sun, fertile soil, good drainage; tolerates high heat, dry conditions. Propagate by seed and division.

USES: Edging beds and borders; rock gardens.

COREOPSIS VERTICILLATA

COMMON NAME: Tickseed, thread-leaf coreopsis

FAMILY: Compositae (Daisies)

DESCRIPTION: Native to the southern United States. Plants form low, spreading clumps of small, narrow green leaves and wiry stems covered with masses of 2-inch (5cm), star-shaped flowers. Summer-flowering.

HEIGHT: 1½ to 2 feet (.5 to .6m).

COLOR: Golden yellow, lemon yellow.

HARDINESS: Zones 4 to 9.

CULTURE: Very easy to grow in full sun; needs good drainage; tolerates poor soil, drought. Propagate by root division and seed.

USES: Massing in beds and borders. Good accent in rock gardens and along dry walls.

CORONILLA VARIA

COMMON NAME: Crown vetch

FAMILY: Leguminosae (Peas)

DESCRIPTION: Native to Europe. Plants resemble mounds of clover; multiple oval green leaflets crowd the square stems, and tight florets form 1-inch (2.5cm) globes. Summer-flowering.

HEIGHT: 2½ feet (.8m).

COLOR: Usually deep pink, but variable through light pink to white.

HARDINESS: Zones 4 to 8.

CULTURE: Prefers full sun and well-drained soil; tolerates dry slopes, poor soil. Propagate by seed either direct-sown or started 10 weeks before outdoor planting. Grows slowly the first season, then spreads aggressively to form a dense groundcover.

USES: Mostly for covering large expanses of dry slopes, especially along driveways and highways.

CORYDALIS CHEILANTHIFOLIA

COMMON NAME: Yellow corydalis

FAMILY: Fumariaceae (Fumitories)

DESCRIPTION: Native to Europe. Plants grow clumps of feathery, blue-green leaves and practically stemless flower spikes with trumpetlike, ½-inch (13mm) blooms. Early spring-flowering.

HEIGHT: To 8 inches (20cm).

COLOR: Yellow.

HARDINESS: Zones 5 to 7.

CULTURE: Grows in sun or shade; requires fertile soil, good drainage. Propagate by division and seed. Difficult to transplant unless started in peat pots.

USES: Mostly woodland gardens; rock gardens, dry walls.

DELPHINIUM ELATUM

COMMON NAME: Delphinium

FAMILY: Ranunculaceae (Buttercups)

DESCRIPTION: Native to Europe. Plants have sharply indented, maplelike green leaves and erect stems studded with 1½-inch (4cm) semidouble flowers, forming a column. Late spring- and autumn-flowering; best when nights are cool. Dwarf forms are also available, growing 1 to 2 feet (.3 to .6m) high.

HEIGHT: 6 feet (1.8m).

COLOR: Blue, white, pink, purple, yellow.

HARDINESS: Zones 2 to 9, depending on variety.

CULTURE: Prefers sun or light shade, well-drained, fertile, loamy soil. Propagate by seed and cuttings. Tall kinds generally need staking to keep the heavy flower stems erect.

USES: Tall accent in mixed beds and borders. Spectacular cut flower.

DIANTHUS DELTOIDES

COMMON NAME: Maiden pink

FAMILY: Caryophyllaceae (Pinks)

DESCRIPTION: Native to Europe. Plants form grasslike clumps of blue-green leaves with masses of dainty, ¼-inch (6mm) flowers. Spring-flowering.

HEIGHT: 6 to 12 inches (15 to 31cm).

COLOR: Pink, red, white, mostly with contrasting "eyes."

HARDINESS: Zones 5 to 8.

CULTURE: Prefers full sun, good drainage; tolerates poor, sandy soil. Propagated by division.

USES: Edging beds and borders; rock gardens, dry walls, cracks in flagstone.

DIANTHUS KNAPPII

COMMON NAME: Yellow cottage pink

FAMILY: Caryophyllaceae (Pinks)

DESCRIPTION: Native to Europe. Plants grow bushy clumps of narrow green leaves and erect stems topped with clusters of ¾-inch (19mm), star-shaped flowers. Late spring- and early summer-flowering, lasting several weeks.

HEIGHT: 12 inches (31cm).

COLOR: Yellow.

HARDINESS: Zones 4 to 8.

CULTURE: Prefers full sun, good drainage, poor soil. Propagated by root division, layering, stem cuttings.

USES: Edging beds and borders; rock gardens, dry walls. Good for cutting.

DIANTHUS PLUMARIUS

COMMON NAME: Cottage pink, grass pink

FAMILY: Caryophyllaceae (Pinks)

DESCRIPTION: Native to Europe and Asia. Plants form grasslike clumps with narrow, blue-green leaves and erect stems topped with fragrant, double flowers to 1 inch (2.5cm), resembling miniature carnations. Late spring-flowering, lasting several weeks.

HEIGHT: 12 to 18 inches (31 to 46cm).

COLOR: Rose, purple, white.

HARDINESS: Zones 4 to 8.

CULTURE: Prefers full sun, fertile, slightly alkaline soil, and good drainage. Propagate by root division, layering, stem cuttings. Short-lived as perennials.

USES: Massing in beds and borders, rock gardens, cutting gardens, especially as an edging.

DICENTRA HYBRIDS

COMMON NAME: Dutchman's-breeches

FAMILY: Fumariaceae (Fumitories)

DESCRIPTION: Hybrids of species native to North America and China. Plants grow compact clumps of finely divided green leaves and erect stems crowded with heart-shaped flowers to 1½ inches (4cm) long. Spring-flowering, continuing through summer.

HEIGHT: 12 to 18 inches (31 to 46cm).

COLOR: Pinkish purple.

HARDINESS: Zones 4 to 8.

CULTURE: Grows in sun or shade; prefers well-drained, humus-rich soil. Propagate by division after flowering.

USES: Excellent massed in woodland gardens; also edging beds and borders.

DICENTRA SPECTABILIS

COMMON NAME: Bleeding-heart, Japanese bleeding-heart

FAMILY: Fumariaceae (Fumitories)

DESCRIPTION: Native to Japan. Shrubby plants grow woody stems featuring lacy, green leaves and arching stems strung with pendant, 1-inch (2.5cm), heart-shaped flowers. Spring-flowering.

HEIGHT: 2 to 3 feet (.6 to .9m).

COLOR: Pink, white.

HARDINESS: Zones 4 to 8.

CULTURE: Grows in sun or light shade; needs humus-rich, moist soil and good drainage. Propagate by root division.

USES: Good accent in mixed beds and borders; rock gardens.

DICTAMNUS ALBUS

COMMON NAME: Dittany, gas plant

FAMILY: Rutaceae (Rues)

DESCRIPTION: Native to Europe and Asia. Plants have small, oval, light green leaflets and erect flower spikes studded with 1-inch (2.5cm) flowers. Vapors emitted by the leaves and flowers can be ignited with a match. Early summer-flowering.

HEIGHT: 2 to 3 feet (.6 to .9m).

COLOR: White, pink, rosy red.

HARDINESS: Zones 3 to 8.

CULTURE: Prefers full sun, fertile soil, good drainage. Propagate by seed and root division, though transplanting divisions is not reliable.

USES: Accent in mixed beds and borders.

DIGITALIS GRANDIFLORA

COMMON NAME: Yellow foxglove

FAMILY: Scrophulariaceae (Figworts)

DESCRIPTION: Native to Europe and Asia. Plants form a rosette of hairy, tonguelike green leaves from which emerges a tall flower spike studded with tubular flowers to 2 inches (5cm) long. Summer-flowering.

HEIGHT: 3 to 4 feet (.9 to 1.2m).

COLOR: Yellow.

HARDINESS: Zones 4 to 9.

CULTURE: Grows in sun or light shade; prefers well-drained, humus-rich soil. Propagate by seed and by root division after flowering.

USES: Massed in mixed beds and borders. Plants are used medicinally but be aware that all parts are considered poisonous.

DODECATHEON MEADIA

COMMON NAME: Shooting-star

FAMILY: Primulaceae (Primroses)

DESCRIPTION: Native to North America, particularly the Pacific Northwest. Rosette-forming plants have tonguelike, pale green leaves and slender, erect stems each topped with a cluster of nodding, 1-inch (2.5cm) flowers. Swept-back petals resemble miniature cyclamen. Spring-flowering.

HEIGHT: 1 to 2 feet (.3 to .6m).

COLOR: White, pink, rosy red.

HARDINESS: Zones 5 to 7.

CULTURE: Prefers a lightly shaded location, well-drained, fertile soil. Propagate by division.

USES: Accent in mixed beds and borders, edging paths in woodland gardens, massed along water features.

DORONICUM PARDALIANCHES (also *D. CORDATUM*)

COMMON NAME: Leopard's-bane

FAMILY: Compositae (Daisies)

DESCRIPTION: Native to Europe. Plants grow erect stems with spear-shaped, bright green leaves and 2-inch (5cm), daisylike flowers. Early spring-flowering.

HEIGHT: 2 feet (.6m).

COLOR: Yellow.

HARDINESS: Zones 4 to 8.

CULTURE: Grows in sun or partial shade; prefers good drainage, humus-rich soil. Propagate by division.

USES: Massed in beds and borders, woodland gardens. Good for cutting. Combines well with tulips.

ECHINACEA PURPUREA

COMMON NAME: Purple coneflower

FAMILY: Compositae (Daisies)

DESCRIPTION: Native to North America. Plants have broad, lancelike, dark green leaves and erect stems topped with 3-inch (7.5cm), daisylike flowers with a buttonlike center. Summer-flowering.

HEIGHT: 3 to 4 feet (.9 to 1.2m).

COLOR: Pink or white with chocolate brown center.

HARDINESS: Zones 4 to 9.

CULTURE: Prefers full sun, well-drained loam or sandy soil; tolerates drought well. Propagate by division.

USES: Excellent for massing in mixed beds and borders. Suitable for cutting. Combines well with rudbeckias, especially in meadow wildflower plantings.

ECHINOPS RITRO

COMMON NAME: Small globe thistle

FAMILY: Compositae (Daisies)

DESCRIPTION: Native to Europe and Asia. Thistlelike plants have prickly, sharply indented, glossy green leaves with pale, velvety undersides and erect stems topped with round, golf-ball-size flower clusters. Summer-flowering.

HEIGHT: 4 feet (1.2m).

COLOR: Metallic blue.

HARDINESS: Zones 4 to 9.

CULTURE: Prefers full sun; tolerates poor soil, high heat. Propagate by seed and by division after flowering.

USES: Bold accent in beds and borders, especially as a background to phlox and daylilies.

EPIMEDIUM GRANDIFLORUM

COMMON NAME: Barrenwort

FAMILY: Berberidaceae (Barberries)

DESCRIPTION: Native to Europe. Spreading plants cover the ground with decorative, heart-shaped, light green leaves and masses of nodding, 1-inch (2.5cm) flowers. Spring-flowering; good autumn leaf color.

HEIGHT: 12 inches (31cm).

COLOR: Pink.

HARDINESS: Zones 5 to 9.

CULTURE: Prefers a lightly shaded location and moist, humus-rich soil, though will grow in poor, stony soil, hence its common name. Propagate by division.

USES: Ground cover in woodland gardens; edging paths; massing in rock gardens.

ERIGERON HYBRIDS

COMMON NAME: Fleabane

FAMILY: Compositae (Daisies)

DESCRIPTION: Developed from species native to Europe and North America. Plants form mounded clumps of slender, pointed, gray-green leaves and 2-inch (5cm), daisylike flowers. Early summer-flowering; best when nights are cool.

HEIGHT: 2 feet (.6m).

COLOR: Mostly pink or rosy red with bright yellow center.

HARDINESS: Zones 5 to 8.

CULTURE: Prefers full sun, good drainage. Tolerates salt spray. Propagate by division.

USES: Especially popular in coastal gardens, as an accent in mixed beds and borders, and massed in rock gardens.

ERYNGIUM ALPINUM

COMMON NAME: Eryngo

FAMILY: Umbelliferae (Carrots)

DESCRIPTION: Native to Europe. Thistlelike plants produce many branching stems and sharply indented, glossy green leaves with prickles. The 4-inch (10cm) flowers consist of a dome of florets surrounded by a decorative spiny collar. Summer-flowering.

HEIGHT: 3 to 4 feet (.9 to 1.2m).

COLOR: Metallic blue, white.

HARDINESS: Zones 5 to 8.

CULTURE: Prefers full sun, good drainage; tolerates poor, stony, or sandy soil. Propagate by root cuttings.

USES: Popular in coastal gardens, as an accent in mixed beds and borders, massed in rock gardens. Makes a good dried flower.

EUPHORBIA GRIFFITHII

COMMON NAME: Fire glow euphorbia

FAMILY: Euphorbiaceae (Spurges)

DESCRIPTION: Native to the Himalayas. Clump-forming plants grow erect stems with narrow, pointed, dark green leaves and 4-inch (10cm), rounded, flower clusters. Late spring-flowering.

HEIGHT: 3 feet (.9m).

COLOR: Orange-red.

HARDINESS: Zones 4 to 9.

CULTURE: Prefers full sun, well-drained, humus-rich soil, but tolerates a wide range of poor soils. Propagate by division and stem cuttings.

USES: Accent in mixed beds and borders. Beautiful in rock gardens, especially along rocky stream banks.

EUPHORBIA MYRSINITES

COMMON NAME: Spurge, myrtle euphorbia

FAMILY: Euphorbiaceae (Spurges)

DESCRIPTION: Native to the Mediterranean region. Sprawling plants grow trailing, succulent stems of scalelike, blue-green leaves, tipped with 2-inch (5cm) flower clusters. Early spring-flowering.

HEIGHT: 6 inches (15cm).

COLOR: Bright yellow and lime green.

HARDINESS: Zones 5 to 8.

CULTURE: Prefers full sun; tolerates poor, dry, stony soil but prefers moist, well-drained soil. Propagate by layering and stem cuttings.

USES: Mostly to cover hard-to-plant dry slopes, cracks in flagstone, dry walls; massing in rock gardens.

EUPHORBIA POLYCHROMA (also *E. EPITHYMOIDES*)

COMMON NAME: Spurge, cushion spurge

FAMILY: Euphorbiaceae (Spurges)

DESCRIPTION: Native to the Mediterranean region. Mound-shaped plants grow small, narrow, pointed, bright green leaves in a whorl that forms a collar around 2-inch (5cm) flower clusters. Spring-flowering.

HEIGHT: 12 inches (31cm).

COLOR: Bright yellow.

HARDINESS: Zones 5 to 9.

CULTURE: Prefers full sun, good drainage; tolerates poor soil, high heat. Propagate by division and stem cuttings.

USES: Edging beds and borders; rock gardens.

EUPHORBIA WULFENII

COMMON NAME: Spurge, shrub euphorbia

FAMILY: Euphorbiaceae (Spurges)

DESCRIPTION: Native to the Mediterranean region. Tender plants form massive clumps of succulent, erect stems with narrow, pointed, blue-green leaves and a columnar, 12-inch (31cm) flower cluster of ½-inch (13mm), cup-shaped florets. Spring-flowering.

HEIGHT: 4 to 6 feet (1.2 to 1.8m).

COLOR: Yellow-green.

HARDINESS: Zone 8.

CULTURE: Grows in sun or light shade; tolerates a wide range of soils providing drainage is good. Propagate by division and stem cuttings. Generally needs pruning to the ground in autumn to keep it compact.

USES: Handsome accent in mixed beds and borders, between shrubs along a house foundation.

FILIPENDULA RUBRA

COMMON NAME: Queen-of-the-prairie

FAMILY: Rosaceae (Roses)

DESCRIPTION: Native to North America. Plants grow feathery, five-fingered, serrated green leaves and slender stems topped with a fluffy flower plume resembling cotton candy. Summer-flowering.

HEIGHT: 5 to 6 feet (1.5 to 1.8m).

COLOR: Pink.

HARDINESS: Zones 3 to 8.

CULTURE: Prefers full sun or partial shade, moist soil. Will grow in boggy soils. Propagate by division.

USES: Tall accent in the back of beds and borders.

GAILLARDIA × GRANDIFLORA

COMMON NAME: Blanket flower

FAMILY: Compositae (Daisies)

DESCRIPTION: Native to the southwestern United States. Bushy plants have broad, toothed, dark green leaves and slender, erect stems topped by large daisylike flowers. Dwarf varieties form mounds. Summer-flowering.

HEIGHT: ⅔ to 3 feet (.2 to .9m).

COLOR: Mostly yellow with a dark brown center surrounded by a red zone.

HARDINESS: Zones 4 to 8.

CULTURE: Prefers full sun, good drainage; tolerates poor soil, drought. Propagate by seed and by division after plants have flowered.

USES: Dwarf kinds excellent for edging; tall types good as accents in beds and borders, massing in wildflower meadow gardens.

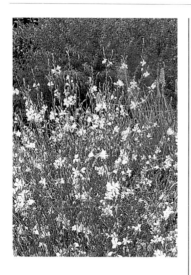

GAURA LINDHEIMERI

COMMON NAME: White gaura

FAMILY: Onagraceae (Evening primroses)

DESCRIPTION: Native to Texas. Bushy plants grow small, oval green leaves and masses of slender, erect stems studded with star-shaped flowers lasting for most of summer.

HEIGHT: 4 to 5 feet (1.2 to 1.5m).

COLOR: White fading to light pink.

HARDINESS: Zones 6 to 9. Needs a protective mulch north of Zone 7.

CULTURE: Prefers full sun, good drainage; tolerates poor soil, drought. Propagate by division in autumn.

USES: Accent in beds and borders.

GENTIANA ACAULIS

COMMON NAME: Stemless gentian, trumpet gentian, alpine gentian

FAMILY: Gentianaceae (Gentians)

DESCRIPTION: Native to the Alps. Plants form low, spreading mounds of straplike, dark green leaves and 2-inch (5cm) long, 1-inch (2.5cm) wide, trumpet-shaped flowers. Spring-flowering.

HEIGHT: To 3 inches (7.5cm).

COLOR: Bright blue.

HARDINESS: Zones 4 to 8.

CULTURE: Prefers sun or light shade, a well-drained gritty or humus-rich soil, cool conditions. Challenging to grow. Propagate by seed and division. A related species, autumn-flowering *G. sino-ornata* from China, is easier to grow, though not so brightly colored.

USES: Mostly grown along woodland paths and as drifts in rock gardens.

GERANIUM ENDRESSII

COMMON NAME: Cranesbill, Pyrenees cranesbill

FAMILY: Geraniaceae (Geraniums)

DESCRIPTION: Native to the Pyrenees mountains. Mound-shaped plants with dissected, dark green leaves are covered with 1-inch (2.5cm), star-shaped flowers during cool conditions of spring and early summer.

HEIGHT: 12 to 18 inches (31 to 46cm).

COLOR: Light pink.

HARDINESS: Zones 4 to 8.

CULTURE: Prefers full sun, good drainage; fertile soil promotes heavier bloom. Best to propagate by division after flowering.

USES: Low accent in beds and borders; massing as a ground cover.

GERANIUM HIMALAYENSE

COMMON NAME: Blue cranesbill

FAMILY: Geraniaceae (Geraniums)

DESCRIPTION: Native to the Himalayas. Mound-shaped plants grow dissected, ivy-shaped green leaves and 2-inch (5cm), cup-shaped flowers. Early summer-flowering.

HEIGHT: 12 to 18 inches (31 to 46cm).

COLOR: Light blue.

HARDINESS: Zones 4 to 8.

CULTURE: Prefers full sun, well-drained, fertile soil, cool nights. Where summers are hot, plants benefit from light shade. Propagate by division after flowering.

USES: Low accent in beds and borders, dry walls, rock gardens.

GERANIUM PSILOSTEMON

COMMON NAME: Cranesbill, Armenian cranesbill

FAMILY: Geraniaceae (Geraniums)

DESCRIPTION: Native to Russia. Bushy plants have indented, maple-shaped green leaves topped with cup-shaped flowers 1½ inches (4cm) across. Early summer-flowering.

HEIGHT: 3 feet (.9m).

COLOR: Magenta marked in the center with a black "eye."

HARDINESS: Zones 4 to 9.

CULTURE: Prefers full sun, good drainage, cool nights. Best to propagate by division after flowering.

USES: Accent in mixed beds and borders.

GERANIUM SANGUINEUM

COMMON NAME: Cranesbill, blood-red cranesbill

FAMILY: Geraniaceae (Geraniums)

DESCRIPTION: Native to Europe. Mound-shaped plants grow heavily indented, dark green leaves covered with 1-inch (2.5cm), cup-shaped flowers. Late spring- and early summer-flowering when nights are cool.

HEIGHT: 12 to 18 inches (31 to 46cm).

COLOR: Rosy red, pale pink, white.

HARDINESS: Zones 4 to 8.

CULTURE: Prefers full sun, well-drained, fertile soil. Propagate by division after flowering.

USES: Edging beds and borders, massing as a ground cover.

GEUM QUELLYON (also *G. CHILENSE*)

COMMON NAME: Avens

FAMILY: Rosaceae (Roses)

DESCRIPTION: Native to Chile. Bushy plants have sharply indented green leaves and erect, loosely branching stems topped with clusters of 1½-inch (4cm) single or double flowers. Late spring- or early summer-flowering; best during cool weather.

HEIGHT: 2½ feet (.8m).

COLOR: Red, orange, yellow.

HARDINESS: Zones 5 to 9.

CULTURE: Prefers full sun or light shade, good drainage. Propagate by division after flowering.

USES: Good accent in mixed beds and borders.

GONIOLIMON TATARICUM (also *LYMONIUM TATARICUM*)

COMMON NAME: German statice

FAMILY: Plumbaginaceae (Plumbagos)

DESCRIPTION: Native to southern Europe and Asia. Plants create a dense clump of narrow, pointed green leaves covered with myriads of tiny, papery, starlike flowers. Midsummer-flowering.

HEIGHT: 18 inches (46cm).

COLOR: White.

HARDINESS: Zones 4 to 8.

CULTURE: Prefers full sun, good drainage; tolerates poor soil, heat, drought. Best to propagate by seed.

USES: Edging beds and borders. Excellent for cutting and dried flower arrangements. Entire plant can be cut to create an instant bouquet.

GYPSOPHILA PANICULATA

COMMON NAME: Baby's-breath

FAMILY: Caryophyllaceae (Pinks)

DESCRIPTION: Native to Europe. Billowing plants have narrow, pointed green leaves covered with masses of ¼-inch (6mm) flowers on brittle branches. Summer-flowering.

HEIGHT: 3 feet (.9m).

COLOR: White or pinkish to reddish.

HARDINESS: Zones 4 to 9.

CULTURE: Easy to grow in full sun and poor soil but prefers well-drained soil. Propagate by seed and by division after plants flower.

USES: Accent in beds and borders. Effective in rock gardens, dry walls.

HELENIUM AUTUMNALE

COMMON NAME: Sneezeweed, false sunflower

FAMILY: Compositae (Daisies)

DESCRIPTION: Native to North America. Plants grow slender, pointed, dark green leaves and stiff, erect stems topped with dense clusters of 2-inch (5cm), daisylike flowers. Late summer- and early autumn-flowering.

HEIGHT: 5 feet (1.5m).

COLOR: Usually yellow, bronze, bicolored.

HARDINESS: Zones 4 to 8.

CULTURE: Prefers full sun, good drainage; tolerates poor soil. Propagate by division in spring or autumn.

USES: Tall accent in mixed beds and borders. Combines well with ornamental grasses, especially *Miscanthus*.

HELIANTHEMUM NUMMULARIUM

COMMON NAME: Sun rose, rock rose

FAMILY: Cistaceae (Rock roses)

DESCRIPTION: Native to Europe. Low, mounded, spreading plants have narrow, gray-green pointed leaves covered in early spring with masses of 1-inch (2.5cm) flowers with petals the texture of crepe paper.

HEIGHT: 12 inches (31cm).

COLOR: Yellow, pink, orange, red.

HARDINESS: Zones 6 to 8.

CULTURE: Prefers full sun, good drainage; tolerates poor, sandy soil. Propagate by seed and by division after flowering.

USES: Edging beds and borders. Effective in rock gardens and spilling over rock ledges or dry walls.

HELIANTHUS ANGUSTIFOLIUS

COMMON NAME: Swamp sunflower

FAMILY: Compositae (Daisies)

DESCRIPTION: Native to North America. Plants grow erect stems with narrow, pointed green leaves topped by clusters of shimmering, 3-inch (7.5cm), daisylike flowers. Late summer-flowering.

HEIGHT: 5 to 6 feet (1.5 to 1.8m).

COLOR: Yellow.

HARDINESS: Zone 6.

CULTURE: Prefers full sun; tolerates moist, boggy soils. Propagate by seed and by division after flowering.

USES: Effective background highlight in mixed beds and borders; massing in meadow wildflower plantings.

HELIANTHUS × *MULTIFLORUS*

COMMON NAME: Sunflower, perennial sunflower

FAMILY: Compositae (Daisies)

DESCRIPTION: Native to North America. Plants grow erect stems with broad, lancelike, dark green leaves and masses of double, 3-inch (7.5cm) flowers. Summer-flowering.

HEIGHT: 5 to 6 feet (1.5 to 1.8m).

COLOR: Yellow.

HARDINESS: Zones 5 to 9.

CULTURE: Prefers full sun, good drainage. In overly fertile soils, the flower clusters can become top-heavy and may need staking. Propagate by division after flowering.

USES: Good background accent in mixed beds and borders. Suitable for cutting.

HELICHRYSUM PETIOLARE (also *H. PETIOLATUM*)

COMMON NAME: Licorice plant

FAMILY: Compositae (Daisies)

DESCRIPTION: Native to South Africa. Mounded, spreading, tender, shrublike plants have rounded, woolly, silvery leaves that are highly ornamental and fragrant with a licorice aroma. Small, inconspicuous flowers cluster on erect stems. Autumn-flowering.

HEIGHT: To 2 feet (.6m).

COLOR: Creamy white, not showy.

HARDINESS: Zone 10.

CULTURE: Prefers full sun, well-drained sandy soil; tolerates drought well. Propagate by seed or cuttings.

USES: Mostly edging beds and borders. Also a silvery highlight, trailing over the edges of containers and balcony planters, mixed with annuals. Good rock garden accent. Suitable for ground cover.

HELIOPSIS HELIANTHOIDES

COMMON NAME: Oxeye, false sunflower

FAMILY: Compositae (Daisies)

DESCRIPTION: Native to North America. Plants have serrated, lancelike green leaves, and long, stiff stems topped by masses of 2½-inch (6.5cm), daisylike, semi-double flowers. Midsummer-flowering.

HEIGHT: 4 to 5 feet (1.2 to 1.5m).

COLOR: Yellow.

HARDINESS: Zones 4 to 9.

CULTURE: Prefers full sun, good drainage; tolerates poor soil, high heat. Propagate by division after flowering.

USES: Tall accent in mixed beds and borders. Good for cutting.

HELLEBORUS ORIENTALIS

COMMON NAME: Lenten rose

FAMILY: Ranunculaceae (Buttercups)

DESCRIPTION: Native to China. Plants are evergreen with leathery, toothed leaves that resemble pachysandra and nodding, 2-inch (5cm), cup-shaped flowers. Early spring-flowering.

HEIGHT: 12 inches (31cm).

COLOR: Mostly white, pink, or purple flecked towards the petal base.

HARDINESS: Zones 4 to 8.

CULTURE: Prefers a shaded location, humus-rich soil. Needs moisture-retentive but well-drained soil. Best to propagate by seed since plants resent division. Readily self-seeds; much easier to grow than its relative, the Christmas rose (*H. niger*).

USES: Good accent in bulb borders; effective ground cover for woodland gardens.

HEMEROCALLIS HYBRIDS

COMMON NAME: Daylily

FAMILY: Liliaceae (Lilies)

DESCRIPTION: Native to China. Plants form fountainlike clumps of straplike green leaves and large trumpetlike blooms in an extensive color range. Summer-flowering.

HEIGHT: 2 to 3 feet (.6 to .9m).

COLOR: Cream, yellow, orange, pink, red, lavender, bicolors.

HARDINESS: Zones 4 to 9.

CULTURE: Prefers full sun, but tolerates light shade; needs fertile soil, good drainage —otherwise foolproof. Propagate by division after flowering.

USES: Accent in mixed beds and borders; massing to cover poor sites and difficult-to-plant slopes.

HEUCHERA SANGUINEA

COMMON NAME: Coralbells

FAMILY: Saxifragaceae (Saxifrages)

DESCRIPTION: Native to Mexico. Plants form mounds of attractive, ivy-shaped green leaves and stiff stems topped by masses of bell-shaped, ¼-inch (6mm) flowers. Spring-flowering.

HEIGHT: 2 feet (.6m).

COLOR: White, pink, red.

HARDINESS: Zones 4 to 8.

CULTURE: Prefers full sun, but tolerates light shade; likes well-drained, fertile, humus-rich soil. Propagate by division after flowering.

USES: Edging beds and borders; massing as a ground cover, especially along stream banks and pool margins.

IBERIS SEMPERVIRENS

COMMON NAME: Edging candytuft, perennial candytuft

FAMILY: Cruciferae (Mustards)

DESCRIPTION: Native to the Mediterranean region. Plants form mounds of evergreen needlelike leaves and masses of four-petaled flowers borne in 1½-inch (4cm), flat, swirling circular clusters. Early spring-flowering.

HEIGHT: 12 inches (31 cm).

COLOR: White.

HARDINESS: Zones 5 to 9.

CULTURE: Prefers full sun, good drainage; tolerates poor, sandy soil. Best to propagate by division. Best pruned after flowering to keep plants low and bushy.

USES: Edging beds and borders; rock gardens; dry walls. Combines well with yellow alyssum and pink creeping phlox.

INULA ENSIFOLIA

COMMON NAME: Swordleaf inula

FAMILY: Compositae (Daisies)

DESCRIPTION: Native to Europe. Clump-forming plants have narrow, pointed, dark green leaves and erect stems with 1½-inch (4cm), daisylike flowers. Summer-flowering.

HEIGHT: 1 to 2 feet (.3 to .6m).

COLOR: Yellow.

HARDINESS: Zones 4 to 9.

CULTURE: Prefers full sun, good drainage; tolerates poor soil. Propagate by division.

USES: Accent in mixed beds and borders.

IRIS CRISTATA

COMMON NAME: Dwarf crested iris

FAMILY: Iridaceae (Irises)

DESCRIPTION: Native to the eastern United States. Plants form colonies of sword-shaped green leaves and 1½-inch (4cm) flowers. Early spring-flowering.

HEIGHT: 4 to 6 inches (10 to 15cm).

COLOR: Pale blue, white.

HARDINESS: Zones 4 to 9.

CULTURE: Prefers lightly shaded location, humus-rich, moisture-retentive soil. Best to propagate by division.

USES: Mostly edging beds and borders; massing at the edge of paths in woodland gardens. Plants naturalize freely.

IRIS × GERMANICA

COMMON NAME: Flag, bearded iris

FAMILY: Iridaceae (Irises)

DESCRIPTION: Hybrids of species native to Europe. Plants grow clumps of sword-shaped green leaves and erect stems topped with spicily fragrant, six-petaled flowers, up to 5 inches (13cm) wide. The lower petals feature a cluster of powdery stamens called the "beard." Early summer-flowering.

HEIGHT: 3 feet (.9m).

COLOR: White, blue, red, ginger, yellow, black, green, bicolored.

HARDINESS: Zones 4 to 9.

CULTURE: Prefers full sun, fertile soil, good drainage. Propagate by division of the bulbous roots in late summer.

USES: Massing in beds and borders. Good for cutting, though flowers last only a day.

IRIS PSEUDACORUS

COMMON NAME: Yellow iris, flag iris

FAMILY: Iridaceae (Irises)

DESCRIPTION: Native to Europe. Plants have slender, arching, sword-shaped green leaves and erect stems bearing 2-inch (5cm) flowers. Summer-flowering.

HEIGHT: 4 to 5 feet (1.2 to 1.5m).

COLOR: Yellow.

HARDINESS: Zones 4 to 9.

CULTURE: Prefers full sun, permanent immersion in water or boggy soil. Propagate by division after flowering.

USES: Water gardens and along the margins of streams and ponds. Combines well with blue Siberian iris.

KNIPHOFIA UVARIA

COMMON NAME: Poker plant, red-hot-poker

FAMILY: Liliaceae (Lilies)

DESCRIPTION: Native to South Africa. Plants grow clumps of stiff, serrated, pointed green leaves and strong, stout stems topped with tight clusters of funnel-shaped flowers that form a "poker." Some varieties have bicolored flowers up to 6 inches (15cm) long. Mostly early summer-flowering.

HEIGHT: 3 to 4 feet (.9 to 1.2m).

COLOR: Red, yellow.

HARDINESS: Zones 5 to 9.

CULTURE: Prefers full sun, excellent drainage. Needs constantly moist soil in summer. Propagate by seed, division, offsets. In cold-winter areas, mulch crown with straw during cold months to avoid rot.

USES: Good accent in mixed beds and borders.

LAMIASTRUM GALEOBDOLON (also ***GALEOBDOLON LUTEUM***)

COMMON NAME: Yellow archangel

FAMILY: Labiatae (Mints)

DESCRIPTION: Native to Europe. Plants form low, spreading clumps of serrated, spear-shaped, evergreen leaves marked with silver. Clusters of hooded flowers are borne profusely in late spring.

HEIGHT: 12 inches (31cm).

COLOR: Yellow.

HARDINESS: Zone 4.

CULTURE: Grows in sun or light shade. Prefers well-drained soil; tolerates poor soil. Propagate by division and stem cuttings.

USES: Mostly an edging in mixed beds and borders; a decorative ground cover.

LAMIUM MACULATUM

COMMON NAME: Spotted dead nettle

FAMILY: Labiatae (Mints)

DESCRIPTION: Native to Europe. Plants grow spreading clusters of decorative, serrated, spear-shaped green leaves that can be variegated white or gold, depending on variety. Hooded flowers appear in clusters. Spring-flowering.

HEIGHT: 12 inches (31cm).

COLOR: Purple, white.

HARDINESS: Zones 4 to 8.

CULTURE: Prefers full sun to flower well and moist, well-drained soil; tolerates poor soil. Propagate by division and stem cuttings.

USES: Edging beds and borders; creating a decorative ground cover.

LAMPRANTHUS SPECTABILIS

COMMON NAME: Ice plant

FAMILY: Aizoaceae (Carpetweeds)

DESCRIPTION: Native to South Africa. Tender plants form clumps of succulent, narrow, pointed green leaves and irides-cent, 2-inch (5cm), daisylike flowers borne so profusely they almost hide the foliage. Early spring-flowering.

HEIGHT: 12 inches (31cm).

COLOR: Purple, red, gold.

HARDINESS: Zone 10.

CULTURE: Demands full sun (flowers stay closed on cloudy days), dry soils, excellent drainage. Propagate by division after flowering.

USES: Mostly dry walls, dry slopes; massed as an edging along seaside paths.

LATHYRUS LATIFOLIUS

COMMON NAME: Perennial pea

FAMILY: Leguminosae (Peas)

DESCRIPTION: Native to Europe. Plants have vining, jointed stems and tendrils for climbing. Oval green leaves and clusters of 1-inch (2.5cm), pealike flowers resemble sweet peas. Summer-flowering.

HEIGHT: 8 feet (2.4m) if staked.

COLOR: Rose, white.

HARDINESS: Zones 5 to 9.

CULTURE: Prefers full sun, well-drained soil; tolerates poor soil, heat. Propagate by seed and division.

USES: Mostly a slope cover and to disguise chain-link fencing.

LAVANDULA AUGUSTIFOLIA

COMMON NAME: English lavender

FAMILY: Labiatae (Mints)

DESCRIPTION: Native to the Mediterranean region. Mounded plants have needlelike, gray-green leaves and tiny, highly fragrant flowers that form a spike. Summer-flowering.

HEIGHT: 2 to 3 feet (.6 to .9m).

COLOR: Mostly blue, purple, white.

HARDINESS: Zones 6 to 9.

CULTURE: Prefers full sun, excellent drainage, even stony soil. Propagate by seed and division.

USES: Good highlight for mixed beds and borders; herb gardens; rock gardens. Forms a fragrant hedge, especially in coastal gardens.

LEONTOPODIUM ALPINUM

COMMON NAME: Edelweiss

FAMILY: Compositae (Daisies)

DESCRIPTION: Native to the Alps. Plants form low clumps of narrow, pointed, velvety, silvery leaves and woolly flowers arranged in a star shape. Spring-flowering.

HEIGHT: 8 to 12 inches (20 to 31cm).

COLOR: White.

HARDINESS: Zones 4 to 6.

CULTURE: Prefers full sun, gritty, well-drained soil. Propagate by division.

USES: Mostly an edging in mixed beds and borders; rock gardens; trough gardens.

LIGULARIA DENTATA

COMMON NAME: Heartleaf goldenray

FAMILY: Compositae (Daisies)

DESCRIPTION: Native to China and Japan. Clump-forming plants have lustrous, heart-shaped leaves 12 inches (31cm) or more across, some with a bronze sheen. The 1-inch (2.5cm), daisylike flowers are held erect in clusters. Midsummer-flowering.

HEIGHT: 4 feet (1.2m).

COLOR: Orange.

HARDINESS: Zones 4 to 8.

CULTURE: Prefers full sun, moist, loam soil. Propagate by division.

USES: Tall accent for mixed beds and borders. Effective along stream banks and pond margins.

LIGULARIA PRZEWALSKII

COMMON NAME: Rocket ligularia

FAMILY: Compositae (Daisies)

DESCRIPTION: Native to Europe. Plants form clumps of large, serrated, ivy-shaped, green leaves and erect, dark purple stems bearing a 1½-foot (.5m) flower spike. Early summer-flowering.

HEIGHT: 5 to 6 feet (1.5 to 1.8m).

COLOR: Yellow.

HARDINESS: Zones 4 to 8.

CULTURE: Prefers cool conditions in sun or partial shade, humus-rich, well-drained loam soil. Will wilt on hot, sunny days. Propagate by division.

USES: Good for massing as a tall background in mixed beds and borders, along stream banks and pond margins.

LILIUM ASIATIC HYBRIDS

COMMON NAME: Mid-century lilies

FAMILY: Liliaceae (Lilies)

DESCRIPTION: Hybrids of species native to China and Japan. The mid-century hybrids are the easiest to grow of garden lilies, producing long, strong, dark green stems with lancelike leaves and upward-facing, chalice-shaped flowers to 5 inches (13cm) across. Summer-flowering.

HEIGHT: 3 feet (.9m).

COLOR: Red, orange, yellow, pink, purple, white.

HARDINESS: Zones 5 to 8.

CULTURE: Grow in sun or shade in well-drained, humus-rich soil. Propagate by division and bulbils that form in the leaf axils.

USES: Good accent in mixed beds and borders; massing in woodland gardens, where they may naturalize.

LIMONIUM PEREZII

COMMON NAME: Sea lavender, sea statice

FAMILY: Plumbaginaceae (Plumbagos)

DESCRIPTION: Native to Japan. Clump-forming plants have leathery, lettucelike green leaves and erect stems topped by billowing, branching, rounded clusters of ⅛-inch (3mm) papery flowers. Summer-flowering.

HEIGHT: 2 feet (.6m).

COLOR: Purple.

HARDINESS: Zones 9 and 10.

CULTURE: Prefers full sun, well-drained, sandy soil. Tolerates salt spray. Propagate by division.

USES: Massing in mixed beds and borders. Good for coastal gardens in mild-winter areas. Excellent for dried flower arrangements.

LINUM FLAVUM

COMMON NAME: Golden flax

FAMILY: Linaceae (Flax)

DESCRIPTION: Native to Europe. Slender stems with small, oval, green leaves bear 1-inch (2.5cm), star-shaped flowers with shimmering petals. Early summer-flowering.

HEIGHT: 12 inches (31cm).

COLOR: Yellow.

HARDINESS: Zones 5 to 7.

CULTURE: Prefers full sun, good drainage; tolerates poor soil. Propagate by seed and division.

USES: Edging mixed beds and borders; massing in rock gardens.

LINUM PERENNE

COMMON NAME: Perennial flax, blue flax

FAMILY: Linaceae (Flax)

DESCRIPTION: Native to Europe. Plants grow narrow, pointed green leaves and delicate, slender stems topped with shimmering ¾-inch (19mm) flowers. Late spring-flowering.

HEIGHT: 1 to 2 feet (.3 to .6m).

COLOR: Blue.

HARDINESS: Zones 5 to 8.

CULTURE: Prefers full sun, good drainage; tolerates poor soil. Propagate by seed and division.

USES: Mostly massed in mixed beds and borders. A component in wildflower meadow mixtures. A source of linseed oil and fibers for linen.

LIRIOPE MUSCARI

COMMON NAME: Big blue lilyturf

FAMILY: Lilaceae (Lilies)

DESCRIPTION: Native to Asia. Plants form clumps of smooth, slender, grasslike, evergreen leaves that create a fountain effect. Erect stems bear clusters of small flowers. Summer-flowering.

HEIGHT: 12 to 18 inches (31 to 46cm).

COLOR: Lavender-blue.

HARDINESS: Zones 6 to 10.

CULTURE: Grows in sun or light shade; needs fertile soil, good drainage. Propagate by division.

USES: Mostly a ground cover under deciduous trees and as an edging to paths.

LOBELIA CARDINALIS

COMMON NAME: Cardinal flower

FAMILY: Lobeliaceae (Lobelias)

DESCRIPTION: Native to North America. Plants have serrated, lancelike green or red-bronze leaves and long, strong stems topped by flower spikes up to 12 inches (31cm) long. Summer-flowering.

HEIGHT: 4 to 5 feet (1.2 to 1.5m).

COLOR: Scarlet.

HARDINESS: Zones 3 to 9.

CULTURE: Prefers full sun or light shade. Prefers moist garden soil to wet, boggy soil. Will even thrive with roots permanently immersed in water. Propagate by seed and division.

USES: Good accent in mixed beds and borders. Especially attractive along stream banks and pond margins.

LOBELIA SIPHILITICA

COMMON NAME: Great lobelia

FAMILY: Lobeliaceae (Lobelias)

DESCRIPTION: Native to North America. Plants grow clumps of long stems with lancelike green leaves topped by slender flower spikes of small, 1-inch (2.5cm) flowers. Summer-flowering.

HEIGHT: 3 to 4 feet (.9 to 1.2m).

COLOR: Blue.

HARDINESS: Zones 5 to 9.

CULTURE: Prefers sun or light shade, moist, heavy soil. Propagate by seed and division.

USES: Accent in mixed beds and borders. Attractive planted along stream banks and pond margins.

LYCHNIS CHALCEDONICA

COMMON NAME: Maltese-cross

FAMILY: Caryophyllaceae (Pinks)

DESCRIPTION: Native to Siberia. Plants grow erect stems surrounded by spear-shaped, green leaves and bearing 1-inch (2.5cm) flowers in rounded clusters that resemble a Maltese cross. Early summer-flowering.

HEIGHT: 3 feet (.9m).

COLOR: Rose, scarlet, white.

HARDINESS: Zones 4 to 8.

CULTURE: Prefers full sun, reasonably fertile soil, good drainage. Propagate by division.

USES: Tall background accent in mixed beds and borders.

LYCHNIS CORONARIA

COMMON NAME: Mullein pink, rose campion

FAMILY: Caryophyllaceae (Pinks)

DESCRIPTION: Native to southern Europe. Erect plants grow numerous branching stems; lancelike, woolly, silvery leaves; and star-shaped flowers. Summer-flowering.

HEIGHT: 3 feet (.9m).

COLOR: Rose-red.

HARDINESS: Zones 4 to 8.

CULTURE: Prefers full sun, good drainage; tolerates poor soil. Propagate by seed; may flower the first year if started early indoors.

USES: Good accent in mixed beds and borders. Self-sows readily.

LYSIMACHIA CLETHROIDES

COMMON NAME: Gooseneck loosestrife

FAMILY: Primulaceae (Primroses)

DESCRIPTION: Native to Asia. Bushy plants grow lancelike, green leaves and erect, flowering stems. Small, ½-inch (13mm) flowers are clustered in a curious spike with a crook in it like a goose's neck. Summer-flowering.

HEIGHT: 3 to 4 feet (.9 to 1.2m).

COLOR: White.

HARDINESS: Zones 4 to 9.

CULTURE: Prefers full sun, moist, well-drained soil. Propagate by division. Spreads rapidly and can become invasive if not confined by regular division.

USES: Good accent in mixed beds and borders. Suitable for cutting.

LYSIMACHIA PUNCTATA

COMMON NAME: Garden loosestrife, yellow loosestrife

FAMILY: Primulaceae (Primroses)

DESCRIPTION: Native to Europe. Bushy plants produce erect stems with lancelike, green leaves and star-shaped flowers at each leaf node. Late spring-flowering.

HEIGHT: 3 feet (.9m).

COLOR: Yellow.

HARDINESS: Zones 5 to 8.

CULTURE: Prefers full sun; tolerates poor soil. Propagate by division. Does best in moist soil where it will spread rapidly.

USES: Good accent in mixed beds and borders. Effective along stream banks and pond margins.

LYTHRUM SALICARIA

COMMON NAME: Purple loosestrife

FAMILY: Lythraceae (Loosestrifes)

DESCRIPTION: Native to Europe. Plants have escaped into the wild and become a nuisance in wetland areas. Plants produce erect stems with spear-shaped, green leaves and long, tapering flower spikes studded with numerous flowers. Summer-flowering.

HEIGHT: 4 to 6 feet (1.2 to 1.8m).

COLOR: Purple.

HARDINESS: Zones 4 to 9.

CULTURE: Prefers full sun, moist soil; tolerates a wide range of soil types. Propagate by division.

USES: Good accent in mixed beds and borders. Effective along stream banks and pond margins.

MALVA ALCEA

COMMON NAME: Mallow, pink mallow

FAMILY: Malvaceae (Mallows)

DESCRIPTION: Native to Europe. Bushy plants have heavily indented green leaves and shimmering 1- to 2-inch (2.5 to 5cm) flowers resembling miniature hollyhocks. Early summer-flowering.

HEIGHT: 3 to 4 feet (.9 to 1.2m).

COLOR: Pink.

HARDINESS: Zones 4 to 9.

CULTURE: Prefers full sun, good drainage; tolerates poor soil, salt spray. Propagate by division.

USES: Accent in mixed beds and borders, especially in coastal gardens.

MALVA SYLVESTRIS MAURITIANA

COMMON NAME: High mallow, seashore mallow

FAMILY: Malvaceae (Mallows)

DESCRIPTION: Native to coastal areas of Europe. Bushy plants grow erect stems with ivy-shaped, dark green leaves and 1½-inch (4cm), cup-shaped flowers resembling miniature hollyhocks. Summer-flowering.

HEIGHT: 3 feet (.9m).

COLOR: Purple with darker stripes.

HARDINESS: Zones 4 to 9.

CULTURE: Prefers full sun, well-drained soil; tolerates poor soil, salty coastal conditions. Easy to propagate from seed, direct-sown in late summer to flower the following summer.

USES: Good accent in mixed beds and borders. Suitable for cutting.

MECONOPSIS BETONICIFOLIA

COMMON NAME: Blue poppy

FAMILY: Papaveraceae (Poppies)

DESCRIPTION: Native to the Himalayas. Plants grow erect clumps of hairy, oblong green leaves and slender stems topped with sideways-facing or nodding, saucer-shaped, poppylike flowers up to 3 inches (7.5cm) across. Spring-flowering.

HEIGHT: To 5 feet (1.5m).

COLOR: Clear blue with powdery yellow centers.

HARDINESS: Zone 8.

CULTURE: Prefers a lightly shaded location; moist, humus-rich, acid soil; cool conditions. Challenging to grow, except in areas with cool, moist summers. Propagate by seed. Where summers are hot and dry, plants may flower from an autumn planting of mature seedlings.

USES: Woodland gardens, rock gardens; beautiful massed along stream banks and against old stone walls.

MERTENSIA VIRGINICA

COMMON NAME: Bluebells, Virginia bluebells

FAMILY: Boraginaceae (Borages)

DESCRIPTION: Native to the northeastern United States. Plants grow clumps of erect stems with tonguelike green leaves mottled white and nodding clusters of 1-inch (2.5cm), bell-shaped flowers. Spring-flowering.

HEIGHT: 2 feet (.6m).

COLOR: Blue.

HARDINESS: Zones 4 to 9.

CULTURE: Prefers a lightly shaded location, moist, humus-rich soil. Best to propagate by fresh seed.

USES: Massed as a ground cover in woodland wildflower gardens and as an edging along rustic paths.

MONARDA DIDYMA

COMMON NAME: Bee balm

FAMILY: Labiatae (Mints)

DESCRIPTION: Native to the eastern United States. Plants form bushy clumps of erect stems and spear-shaped green leaves. Hooded flowers arranged in a 2-inch (5cm) circle are attractive to hummingbirds. Summer-flowering.

HEIGHT: 3 to 4 feet (.9 to 1.2m).

COLOR: Red, pink, white.

HARDINESS: Zones 4 to 8.

CULTURE: Prefers full sun, fertile soil, good drainage, though spreads rapidly in moist soil. Propagate by division in spring.

USES: Good accent in mixed beds and borders.

NEPETA × FAASSENII

COMMON NAME: Catmint

FAMILY: Labiatae (Mints)

DESCRIPTION: Hybrid from species native to Europe. Sprawling bushy plants have mintlike, gray-green leaves and masses of small flowers clustered in a tapering spike. Spring-flowering.

HEIGHT: 1 to 2 feet (.3 to .6m).

COLOR: Blue.

HARDINESS: Zones 4 to 8.

CULTURE: Prefers full sun, good drainage; tolerates poor, sandy soil. Propagate by division.

USES: Mostly used as an informal edging to paths and as accents in mixed beds and borders.

NYMPHAEA HYBRIDS

COMMON NAME: Water lily, hardy water lily

FAMILY: Nymphaeaceae (Water lilies)

DESCRIPTION: Developed from species native to Europe and North America. Plants grow only when roots are permanently immersed in water with at least 6 inches (15cm) of depth. Rounded leaves and star-shaped, sometimes fragrant flowers float on the surface. Flower size and leaf colors vary. Summer-flowering.

HEIGHT: To 3 feet (.9m).

COLOR: White, yellow, pink, red, orange.

HARDINESS: Zones vary depending on individual variety, mostly 5 to 9.

CULTURE: Prefers full sun, water temperature above 70°F (21°C) in summer. Roots prefer to be planted in clay soil or, if muskrats are a problem, in sunken containers covered with wire mesh. Propagate by root division.

USES: Used as decoration in pools and ponds. Miniature varieties can be grown in water troughs and tubs.

OENOTHERA FRUTICOSA

COMMON NAME: Sundrops

FAMILY: Onagraceae (Evening primroses)

DESCRIPTION: Native to the eastern United States. Plants form low, spreading clumps of reddish erect stems with narrow, pointed green leaves and shimmering 2-inch (5cm), cup-shaped flowers. Extremely free-flowering in early summer.

HEIGHT: 12 to 18 inches (31 to 46cm).

COLOR: Yellow.

HARDINESS: Zones 5 to 8.

CULTURE: Prefers full sun, good drainage; tolerates poor, sandy soil, heat, drought. Propagate by division.

USES: Good accent massed in mixed beds and borders.

OENOTHERA MISSOURENSIS

COMMON NAME: Evening primrose, Missouri evening primrose

FAMILY: Onagraceae (Evening primroses)

DESCRIPTION: Native to the southern and midwestern United States. Low, sprawling plants grow lancelike silvery leaves and 4-inch (10cm), four-petaled, cup-shaped flowers that open at night and remain open through the day. Summer-flowering.

HEIGHT: 6 inches (15cm).

COLOR: Shimmering, transluscent yellow. Flowers display attractive pink bud sheaths.

HARDINESS: Zones 5 to 8.

CULTURE: Prefers full sun; demands good drainage; tolerates poor soil, dry slopes. Very easy to grow from seed, direct-sown.

USES: Best massed in clumps as an edging to beds and borders or as a colorful accent in rock gardens.

OPUNTIA HUMIFUSA

COMMON NAME: Prickly pear, hardy prickly pear

FAMILY: Cactaceae (Cacti)

DESCRIPTION: Native to the eastern United States. Plants form spreading clumps of flattened, oval, prickly, succulent evergreen leaves called pads. In early summer the tip of each pad produces numerous shimmering, 3-inch (7.5cm) flowers that develop into attractive red, pear-shaped, edible fruits.

HEIGHT: 12 inches (31cm).

COLOR: Yellow.

HARDINESS: Zones 5 to 10.

CULTURE: Prefers full sun, hot summers, good drainage; tolerates poor, sandy soil. Propagate by division and leaf cuttings. The pads fall limp after frost and appear dead but revive at the onset of warm weather.

USES: Edging beds and borders; an accent in rock gardens.

PAEONIA OFFICINALIS

COMMON NAME: Peony, common peony

FAMILY: Paeoniaceae (Peonies)

DESCRIPTION: Native to China. Bushy plants produce branching stems with in-dented leaves and single or double flowers up to 6 inches (15cm) across. Leaf color varies depending on variety. Spring-flowering.

HEIGHT: 3 feet (.9m).

COLOR: Red, pink, white, bicolors.

HARDINESS: Zones 4 to 8.

CULTURE: Prefers full sun; fertile, well-drained, humus-rich soil. Propagate by division of the thick, tuberous rootstocks.

USES: Good accent in mixed beds and borders; a "hedge" to line wide paths and driveways. Suitable for cutting.

PAPAVER ORIENTALE

COMMON NAME: Oriental poppy

FAMILY: Papaveraceae (Poppies)

DESCRIPTION: Native to Asia. Plants form a rosette of hairy, fernlike, indented green leaves. From the center emerges an erect flowering stem topped with a shimmering, 6-inch (15cm), cup-shaped flower. Late spring-flowering.

HEIGHT: 3 to 4 feet (.9 to 1.2m).

COLOR: Red, white, orange, purple, bicolors; usually marked at the petal base with black blotches.

HARDINESS: Zones 4 to 9.

CULTURE: Demands full sun, good drainage. Propagate by seed, division, also root cuttings. Leaves turn brown and plants go dormant during summer.

USES: Good accent massed in mixed beds and borders. Excellent slope cover.

PENSTEMON BARBATUS

COMMON NAME: Beard-tongue, beardlip penstemon

FAMILY: Scrophulariaceae (Figworts)

DESCRIPTION: Native to Mexico and the southwestern United States. Clump-forming plants grow erect stems with slender, lancelike green leaves, topped by a tapering flower spike of 1-inch (2.5cm), tubular flowers attractive to hummingbirds. Early summer-flowering.

HEIGHT: 2 to 3 feet (.6 to .9m).

COLOR: Red.

HARDINESS: Zones 4 to 8.

CULTURE: Prefers full sun or light shade, good drainage; tolerates poor soil. Best to propagate by seed.

USES: Accent in mixed beds and borders, rock gardens.

PEROVSKIA ATRIPLICIFOLIA

COMMON NAME: Russian sage

FAMILY: Labiatae (Mints)

DESCRIPTION: Native to Central Asia. Bushy plants form clusters of fragrant, erect stems with lancelike, silvery green leaves and large tapering spikes of small flowers. Late summer-flowering.

HEIGHT: 3 to 5 feet (.9 to 1.5m).

COLOR: Blue.

HARDINESS: Zones 6 to 9.

CULTURE: Prefers full sun, good drainage; tolerates poor, sandy soil. Propagate by division. Best cut to the ground after flowering to promote new, vigorous growth.

USES: Spectacular accent in mixed beds and borders. Combines well with ornamental grasses.

PHLOMIS FRUTICOSA

COMMON NAME: Jerusalem sage

FAMILY: Labiatae (Mints)

DESCRIPTION: Native to the Mediterranean region. Clump-forming plants grow erect stems with lancelike, woolly green leaves and a circle of hooded flowers at each leaf axil. Early summer-flowering.

HEIGHT: 3 feet (.9m).

COLOR: Yellow.

HARDINESS: Zones 8 to 10.

CULTURE: Prefers full sun, good drainage; tolerates poor, sandy soil. Propagate by division.

USES: Good accent in mixed beds and borders.

PHLOX DIVARICATA

COMMON NAME: Wild blue phlox

FAMILY: Polemoniaceae (Phlox)

DESCRIPTION: Native to the northeastern United States. Creeping plants have upright stems, lancelike, green leaves, and star-shaped flowers to 1½ inches (4cm) across borne in loose clusters. Early summer-flowering.

HEIGHT: 12 to 18 inches (31 to 46cm).

COLOR: Blue, mauve.

HARDINESS: Zones 4 to 8.

CULTURE: Grows in sun or light shade; prefers humus-rich, well-drained soil.

USES: Edging paths and mixed beds and borders; massing in woodland gardens. Especially beautiful underplanted in a bed of tulips.

PHLOX MACULATA

COMMON NAME: Wild phlox

FAMILY: Polemoniaceae (Phlox)

DESCRIPTION: Native to North America. Plants resemble common summer phlox but are earlier flowering (late spring) and not as tall. Possesses oval green leaves; flowers are held erect in tight, 3-inch (7.5cm) clusters.

HEIGHT: To 5 feet (1.5m).

COLOR: Purple, to pink or white.

HARDINESS: Zones 4 to 8.

CULTURE: Prefers full sun, humus-rich, well-drained loam soil. Propagate by division.

USES: Good accent in mixed beds and borders.

PHLOX PANICULATA

COMMON NAME: Perennial phlox, summer phlox

FAMILY: Polemoniaceae (Phlox)

DESCRIPTION: Native to the northeastern United States. Clump-forming plants grow stiff, erect stems with spear-shaped, dark green leaves and 4- to 5-inch (10 to 13cm) clusters of 1-inch (2.5cm), star-shaped flowers. Summer-flowering.

HEIGHT: To 6 feet (1.8cm).

COLOR: Red, pink, white, blue, bicolors.

HARDINESS: Zones 4 to 8.

CULTURE: Prefers full sun, humus-rich loam soil. Propagate by division. Highly susceptible to mildew, which can be controlled by fungicidal sprays.

USES: Tall accent in mixed beds and borders. Good companion to daylilies.

PHLOX SUBULATA

COMMON NAME: Moss pink, mountain pink

FAMILY: Polemoniaceae (Phlox)

DESCRIPTION: Native to North America. Plants form a dense evergreen carpet of needlelike, gray-green leaves covered with masses of tightly packed, ½-inch (13mm), star-shaped flowers. Early spring-flowering.

HEIGHT: 4 to 6 inches (10 to 15cm).

COLOR: Red, pink, white, blue.

HARDINESS: Zones 4 to 9.

CULTURE: Prefers full sun, good drainage; tolerates poor, stony soil. Propagate by division.

USES: Edging mixed beds and borders; rock gardens, dry walls, cracks in flagstone.

PHORMIUM TENAX

COMMON NAME: New Zealand flax

FAMILY: Agavaceae (Agaves)

DESCRIPTION: Native to New Zealand. Tender plants grow a fountain of erect, slender, sword-shaped green or bronze leaves. Usually a foliage accent since the flowers are small and unappealing. Summer-flowering.

HEIGHT: To 6 feet (1.8m).

COLOR: Leaves are usually red-and-green bicolored. Flowers are red, not ornamental.

HARDINESS: Zones 9 to 10.

CULTURE: Prefers full sun; tolerates poor soil, dry conditions. Best to propagate by division.

USES: Invaluable in Mediterranean-style gardens as a foliage accent in beds and borders. Suitable for containers in cold-winter climates where it can be moved indoors during winter. Combines well with ornamental grasses.

PHYSALIS ALKEKENGI

COMMON NAME: Chinese-lantern

FAMILY: Solanaceae (Nightshades)

DESCRIPTION: Native to Asia. Erect plants produce spreading underground stems that can become invasive. Leaves are lancelike, dark green. Small, star-shaped flowers appearing in summer produce golf-ball-size decorative seed cases containing an edible berry in autumn.

HEIGHT: To 2 feet (.6m).

COLOR: Flowers are white and inconspicuous; lanterns are orange or orange-red depending on variety.

HARDINESS: Zones 5 to 8.

CULTURE: Prefers full sun, sandy or loam soil. Grow from seed, for plants will flower and set fruit the first year; can also propagate by root division.

USES: Mostly grown in herb gardens and cutting gardens. Dried seed cases used for arrangements.

PHYSOSTEGIA VIRGINIANA

COMMON NAME: Obedience plant

FAMILY: Labiatae (Mints)

DESCRIPTION: Native to the northeastern United States. Clump-forming plants grow erect stems with lancelike green leaves and tapering flower spikes of snapdragonlike, tubular flowers. The individual florets can be pushed from one side to another and will stay in place, hence the common name. Late summer-flowering.

HEIGHT: 2 to 4 feet (.6 to 1.2m).

COLOR: Pink, white.

HARDINESS: Zones 4 to 8.

CULTURE: Prefers full sun, good drainage; tolerates poor, sandy soil. Propagate by division.

USES: Good accent in mixed beds and borders.

POLEMONIUM REPTANS

COMMON NAME: Jacob's-ladder

FAMILY: Polemoniaceae (Phlox)

DESCRIPTION: Native to the eastern United States. Low, bushy, spreading plants grow clusters of small, pointed green leaflets and loose clusters of ½-inch (13mm), cup-shaped flowers. Late spring- and early summer-flowering.

HEIGHT: 12 inches (31cm).

COLOR: Light blue.

HARDINESS: Zones 4 to 8.

CULTURE: Prefers light shade and humus-rich, well-drained loam soil. Propagate by division.

USES: Edging beds and borders; massing along woodland paths and pond margins.

POLYGONATUM ODORATUM THUNBERGII

COMMON NAME: Solomon's-seal, King-Solomon's-seal

FAMILY: Liliaceae (Lilies)

DESCRIPTION: Native to Japan. Slender, arching stems have lancelike leaves evenly spaced in pairs and small, drooping, bell-shaped flowers to ⅞ inches (22mm) long. Leaves are dark green or cream-and-green variegated depending on variety. Spring-flowering.

HEIGHT: To 3 feet (.9m).

COLOR: Mostly grown for foliage effect. Flowers are white and inconspicuous.

HARDINESS: Zones 4 to 9.

CULTURE: Grows best in shade; prefers humus-rich, well-drained soil. Propagate by root division in spring or autumn.

USES: Invaluable for shade gardens, massed as an accent between ferns, hostas, and shade-tolerant shrubs such as *Enkianthus* and azaleas.

POLYGONUM BISTORTA

COMMON NAME: Snakeweed, bistort

FAMILY: Polygonaceae (Buckwheats)

DESCRIPTION: Native to Europe. Clump-forming plants have leathery, tonguelike green leaves and erect stems topped by a pokerlike flower spike. Early summer-flowering.

HEIGHT: 2 to 3 feet (.6 to .9m).

COLOR: Pink.

HARDINESS: Zones 4 to 8.

CULTURE: Prefers full sun or light shade where summers are hot; tolerates moist soil and poor, sandy soil. Propagate by division.

USES: Accent in mixed beds and borders; edging paths and pond margins.

PRIMULA ALPICOLA

COMMON NAME: Moonlight primrose

FAMILY: Primulaceae (Primroses)

DESCRIPTION: Native to the Himalayas. Plants grow broad, oval, dark green leaves and clusters of nodding, cowsliplike flowers on erect stems held high above the foliage. Spring-flowering.

HEIGHT: To 3 feet (.9m).

COLOR: Yellow to white.

HARDINESS: Zones 6 to 8.

CULTURE: Prefers sun or light shade, moist, humus-rich soil. Needs a cool environment; mostly seen in moist coastal locations. Propagate by seed and division.

USES: Good accent massed along stream banks and pond margins.

PRIMULA × BULLESIANA

COMMON NAME: Bees hybrid primrose

FAMILY: Primulaceae (Primroses)

DESCRIPTION: A cross between species native to China. Plants grow rosettes of oval, crinkled green leaves and slender, erect stems held well above the foliage. Flowers bloom in clusters along the stems. Spring-flowering.

HEIGHT: 2 feet (.6m).

COLOR: Yellow, orange, pink, red, purple.

HARDINESS: Zone 8.

CULTURE: Prefers sun or light shade, moist, humus-rich soil. Needs a cool environment; mostly grown in moist coastal locations. Propagate by seed and division.

USES: Sensational massed along stream banks and pond margins.

PRIMULA JAPONICA

COMMON NAME: Japanese primrose, candelabra primrose

FAMILY: Primulaceae (Primroses)

DESCRIPTION: Native to Japan. Plants form rosettes of crinkled, tongue-like green leaves and slender, erect flower stems. Several clusters of primroselike flowers surround the topmost leaf axils. Spring-flowering.

HEIGHT: 12 to 18 inches (31 to 46cm).

COLOR: Pink, white, magenta, bicolors.

HARDINESS: Zones 6 to 8.

CULTURE: Prefers sun or light shade, constantly moist, humus-rich soil. Propagate by division.

USES: Superb massed in boggy soil along stream banks and pond margins.

PRIMULA VERIS

COMMON NAME: Cowslip, English cowslip

FAMILY: Primulaceae (Primroses)

DESCRIPTION: Native to Europe. Plants form rosettes of crinkled, spear-shaped green leaves and erect stems topped with a nodding cluster of ½-inch (13mm), bell-shaped flowers. Early spring-flowering.

HEIGHT: 8 to 10 inches (20 to 25cm).

COLOR: Yellow, orange, bronze.

HARDINESS: Zones 3 to 8.

CULTURE: Prefers sun or light shade, well-drained, humus-rich soil. Propagate by division.

USES: Edging rustic paths in woodland gardens; edging tulip beds.

PRIMULA VULGARIS

COMMON NAME: English primrose

FAMILY: Primulaceae (Primroses)

DESCRIPTION: Native to Europe. Plants form a rosette of crinkled, spear-shaped leaves and numerous 1½-inch (4cm) single flowers. Early spring-flowering.

HEIGHT: 6 inches (15cm).

COLOR: Yellow.

HARDINESS: Zones 3 to 8.

CULTURE: Prefers full sun or light shade, moist, humus-rich soil. May need mulching to prevent burning where summers are hot. Best to propagate by division.

USES: Edging beds and borders; massing in woodland gardens. Combines well with tulips, ferns, early rhododendrons.

PULMONARIA ANGUSTIFOLIA

COMMON NAME: Lungwort

FAMILY: Boraginaceae (Borages)

DESCRIPTION: Native to Europe. Plants grow clumps of spear-shaped green leaves and clusters of ½-inch (13mm), nodding, bell-shaped flowers resembling English cowslips. Early spring-flowering.

HEIGHT: 12 inches (31cm).

COLOR: Blue.

HARDINESS: Zones 4 to 8.

CULTURE: Grows in sun or partial shade; prefers moist, but well-drained soil. Tolerates poor soil. Propagate by division.

USES: Edging beds and borders; massing along paths in woodland gardens.

PULSATILLA VULGARIS (also *ANEMONE PULSATILLA*)

COMMON NAME: Pasque-flower

FAMILY: Ranunculaceae (Buttercups)

DESCRIPTION: Native to Europe. Plants grow compact clumps of wispy, threadlike leaves covered with a woolly, silvery down. Flowers are cup-shaped, 2 inches (5cm) across. Spring-flowering.

HEIGHT: 12 inches (31cm).

COLOR: Purple with conspicuous orange center.

HARDINESS: Zones 5 to 7.

CULTURE: Prefers full sun, well-drained alkaline soil. Propagate by seed or division in spring.

USES: Mostly rock gardens.

RODGERSIA AESCULIFOLIA

COMMON NAME: Rodgers flower

FAMILY: Saxifragaceae (Saxifrages)

DESCRIPTION: Native to China. Bushy, spreading plants grow large, five-fingered, heavily textured, lustrous green leaves and dramatic flower plumes on erect stems. *R. podophylla* is a bronze-leaf form. Summer-flowering.

HEIGHT: To 6 feet (1.8m).

COLOR: Creamy white to pink.

HARDINESS: Zones 5 to 8.

CULTURE: Prefers full sun or light shade, moist, humus-rich soil. Best to propagate by division in spring.

USES: Beautiful as an accent massed along stream banks and pond margins.

RUDBECKIA FULGIDA

COMMON NAME: Black-eyed Susan

FAMILY: Compositae (Daisies)

DESCRIPTION: Native to North America. Plants form clumps of lancelike, dark green leaves and masses of 3-inch (7.5cm), daisylike flowers with black centers. Summer-flowering.

HEIGHT: 3 feet (.9m).

COLOR: Yellow.

HARDINESS: Zones 4 to 9.

CULTURE: Prefers full sun, good drainage; tolerates poor soil. Best to propagate by division.

USES: Accent in mixed beds and borders; massing along slopes for erosion control. Good companion to ornamental grasses.

SALVIA PRATENSIS

COMMON NAME: Meadow clary

FAMILY: Labiatae (Mints)

DESCRIPTION: Native to Europe. Plants form spreading clumps of spear-shaped, dark green leaves and erect stems with long, tapering flower spikes. Early summer-flowering.

HEIGHT: 3 feet (.9m).

COLOR: Lavender-blue.

HARDINESS: Zones 6 to 8.

CULTURE: Prefers full sun, fertile soil, good drainage. Best to propagate by division.

USES: Accent in beds and borders. Good for massing to fill an entire island bed or edge a path.

SALVIA SCLAREA

COMMON NAME: Clary

FAMILY: Labiatae (Mints)

DESCRIPTION: Native to the Mediterranean region. Actually a biennial, this plant is frequently used in perennial borders as a tall accent. Plants grow bushy with thick, velvety, heart-shaped green leaves and long, slender, erect stems topped with large flower spikes. Early summer-flowering.

HEIGHT: To 4 feet (1.2m).

COLOR: Lilac, pink, white.

HARDINESS: Zones 5 to 8.

CULTURE: Prefers full sun, well-drained loam or sandy soil. Sow seeds directly into the garden in spring or early summer for late-spring to early-summer flowering the following season.

USES: Effective massed as a background to beds and borders. Combines well with tall hollyhocks. A fragrant oil extract is used medicinally, so the plant is often included in herb gardens.

SALVIA × SUPERBA

COMMON NAME: Violet sage

FAMILY: Labiatae (Mints)

DESCRIPTION: A hybrid of species native to Europe. Plants grow bushy with spear-shaped green leaves and dense flower spikes up to 12 inches (31cm) long. Early summer-flowering.

HEIGHT: To 2½ feet (.8m).

COLOR: Dark violet-blue.

HARDINESS: Zones 5 to 9.

CULTURE: Prefers full sun, well-drained loam or sandy soil. Propagate by division and cuttings.

USES: Good accent in mixed beds and borders.

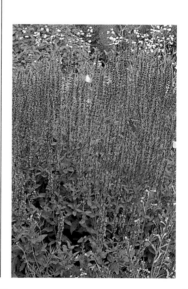

SANTOLINA CHAMAECYPARISSUS

COMMON NAME: Lavender cotton

FAMILY: Compositae (Daisies)

DESCRIPTION: Native to southern Europe. Fragrant, cypresslike, silvery evergreen foliage forms a neat mound with masses of ½-inch (13mm), buttonlike flowers. Midsummer-flowering.

HEIGHT: 2 feet (.6m).

COLOR: Yellow.

HARDINESS: Zones 6 to 9.

CULTURE: Prefers full sun, good drainage; tolerates poor, sandy soil, heat, drought. Propagate by division.

USES: Good for edging beds and borders. Can be pruned heavily to create a neat hedge, though this prevents flowering. A green-leafed variety, *S. virens*, is often used in combination to create "knot garden" designs.

SAPONARIA OCYMOIDES

COMMON NAME: Soapwort, rock soapwort

FAMILY: Caryophyllaceae (Pinks)

DESCRIPTION: Native to the Mediterranean region. Plants form a low, spreading carpet of tiny, spear-shaped bright green leaves, covered in spring with masses of star-shaped flowers to ½ inch (13mm).

HEIGHT: 3 to 4 inches (7.5 to 10cm).

COLOR: Deep pink.

HARDINESS: Zones 4 to 8.

CULTURE: Prefers full sun, good drainage; tolerates poor, sandy soil. Propagate by division.

USES: Good for edging beds and borders; rock gardens, dry walls, dry slopes, cracks in flagstone.

SCABIOSA CAUCASICA

COMMON NAME: Scabious, pincushion flower

FAMILY: Dipsacaceae (Teasels)

DESCRIPTION: Native to Europe. Clump-forming plants grow toothed green leaves and erect stems topped with a flat, rounded, 3- to 4-inch (7.5 to 10cm) flower with a center crest resembling a pincushion. Early summer-flowering.

HEIGHT: 2½ to 3 feet (.8 to .9m).

COLOR: Blue, white.

HARDINESS: Zones 4 to 9.

CULTURE: Prefers full sun, good drainage; tolerates poor, sandy soil. Propagate by division.

USES: Accent in beds and borders. Excellent for cutting.

SEDUM ACRE

COMMON NAME: Golden-carpet, yellow sedum

FAMILY: Crassulaceae (Orpines)

DESCRIPTION: Native to Europe and Asia. Plants produce a low, spreading carpet of small, pointed, beadlike pale green leaves covered with masses of tiny star-shaped flowers. Early spring-flowering.

HEIGHT: 3 inches (7.5cm).

COLOR: Yellow.

HARDINESS: Zones 4 to 9.

CULTURE: Prefers full sun, good drainage; tolerates poor, stony soil, high heat. Propagate by division.

USES: Ground cover for dry slopes; edging beds and borders; dry walls, cracks in flagstone, rock gardens.

SEDUM × 'AUTUMN JOY'

COMMON NAME: Hybrid stonecrop

FAMILY: Crassulaceae (Orpines)

DESCRIPTION: A cross between species native to China. Clump-forming plants grow fleshy, oval green leaves around erect stems each topped with a 4-inch (10cm), mounded, broccoli-like cluster of flowers. Late summer-flowering, holding color to the end of autumn.

HEIGHT: 2½ feet (.8m).

COLOR: Deep pink to rusty red.

HARDINESS: Zones 4 to 9.

CULTURE: Prefers full sun; tolerates poor soil, from dry, sandy soil to constantly wet conditions. Withstands heat, drought. Propagate by cuttings and division.

USES: Good accent in mixed beds and borders. Popular planted in rock gardens and combined with ornamental grasses.

SEDUM BREVIFOLIUM

COMMON NAME: Stonecrop, white stonecrop

FAMILY: Crassulaceae (Orpines)

DESCRIPTION: Native to the Mediterranean region. Low-growing, compact, spreading plants bear clusters of small star-shaped flowers and fleshy, beadlike leaves. Early summer-flowering.

HEIGHT: To 6 inches (15cm).

COLOR: White.

HARDINESS: Zones 5 to 8.

CULTURE: Prefers full sun, well-drained sandy or loam soil; tolerates heat, drought. Best to propagate by leaf cuttings, stem cuttings, division.

USES: Rock gardens; edging beds and borders.

SEDUM KAMTSCHATICUM

COMMON NAME: Stonecrop, orange stonecrop

FAMILY: Crassulaceae (Orpines)

DESCRIPTION: Native to Asia. Plants are low and spreading with shiny, oval, scalloped green leaves and masses of flat clusters of star-shaped florets from ⅝ to ¾ inch (16 to 19mm) wide. Summer-flowering.

HEIGHT: To 12 inches (31cm).

COLOR: Mostly yellow, sometimes with an orange tint.

HARDINESS: Zones 4 to 9.

CULTURE: Prefers full sun, well-drained sandy or loam soil; tolerates heat, drought. Best to propagate by leaf cuttings, stem cuttings, division.

USES: Edging beds and borders. Good flowering ground cover for dry places.

SEDUM MAXIMUM

COMMON NAME: Stonecrop, great stonecrop

FAMILY: Crassulaceae (Orpines)

DESCRIPTION: Native to Europe and Asia. Plants grow sprawling mounds of fleshy, lancelike green leaves on branching stems and masses of tight, flat flower clusters. Summer-flowering. The variety 'Atropurpureum' has glossy, bronze-colored foliage.

HEIGHT: 1 to 3 feet (.3 to .9m).

COLOR: Pink.

HARDINESS: Zones 4 to 8.

CULTURE: Prefers full sun, good drainage; tolerates poor soil, heat, drought. Propagate by leaf cuttings, stem cuttings, division.

USES: Mostly edging beds and borders.

SEDUM SPURIUM

COMMON NAME: Stonecrop, dragon's blood

FAMILY: Crassulaceae (Orpines)

DESCRIPTION: Native to Asia. Low, spreading, succulent plants grow small, pointed, beadlike green leaves and masses of small starry flowers. Summer-flowering.

HEIGHT: 6 inches (15cm).

COLOR: Rosy red.

HARDINESS: Zones 4 to 9.

CULTURE: Prefers full sun, good drainage; tolerates poor, stony soil, high heat. Propagate by division.

USES: Ground cover for dry slopes; edging beds and borders; dry walls, rock gardens.

SISYRINCHIUM STRIATUM

COMMON NAME: Yellow-eyed grass

FAMILY: Iridaceae (Irises)

DESCRIPTION: Native to Chile. Plants grow clumps of irislike, sword-shaped gray-green leaves and strong, erect stems studded with flowers, forming a columnar flower spike. Early summer-flowering.

HEIGHT: 2 to 3 feet (.6 to .9m).

COLOR: Creamy yellow.

HARDINESS: Zones 7 to 8.

CULTURE: Prefers full sun; tolerates moist, boggy soil. Propagate by seed or by division after flowering.

USES: Good accent in mixed beds and borders. Effective along stream banks and pond margins.

SOLIDAGO HYBRIDS

COMMON NAME: Goldenrod

FAMILY: Compositae (Daisies)

DESCRIPTION: Crosses between species mostly native to North America. Plants grow clumps of erect stems with spear-shaped green leaves and tapering, 12-inch (31cm) flower spikes massed with tiny, daisylike flowers. Midsummer-flowering.

HEIGHT: 2 to 4 feet (.6 to 1.2m).

COLOR: Golden yellow.

HARDINESS: Zones 4 to 9.

CULTURE: Prefers full sun; tolerates poor soil, heat, drought. Propagate by division.

USES: Good accent in mixed beds and borders. Excellent companion to ornamental grasses. Though the wild species can be invasive and weedy, the garden hybrids are well-behaved and striking.

STACHYS BYZANTINA (also *S. OLYMPICA*)

COMMON NAME: Woolly betony, lamb's-ears

FAMILY: Labiatae (Mints)

DESCRIPTION: Native to eastern Europe. Plants form low, spreading cushions of broad, spear-shaped, woolly, silvery leaves and erect, tapering flower spikes with small, 1-inch (2.5cm) flowers. Summer-flowering.

HEIGHT: 1 to 2 feet (.3 to .6m).

COLOR: Purple.

HARDINESS: Zones 4 to 9.

CULTURE: Prefers full sun, good drainage; tolerates poor soil, heat, drought. Propagate by division.

USES: Good accent or edging in beds and borders. Effective in all-white theme gardens and as a ground cover.

STOKESIA LAEVIS (also *S. CYANEA*)

COMMON NAME: Stokes' aster

FAMILY: Compositae (Daisies)

DESCRIPTION: Native to North America. Plants form clumps of narrow, pointed dark green leaves and 3-inch (7.5cm), cornflowerlike flowers. Summer-flowering.

HEIGHT: 2 feet (.6m).

COLOR: Lavender-blue.

HARDINESS: Zones 5 to 8. Mulching is advisable for winter protection.

CULTURE: Prefers full sun, fertile soil, good drainage. Propagate by seed or division.

USES: Good accent in mixed beds and borders.

TANACETUM COCCINEUM (also *CHRYSANTHEMUM COCCINEUM*)

COMMON NAME: Pyrethum, painted daisy

FAMILY: Compositae (Daisies)

DESCRIPTION: Native to Africa. Plants have fernlike green leaves and slender stems topped with 2- to 3-inch (5 to 7.5cm), daisylike flowers. Late spring-flowering.

HEIGHT: 2 to 3 feet (.6 to .9m).

COLOR: Red, pink, white.

HARDINESS: Zones 5 to 9.

CULTURE: Prefers full sun, well-drained, fertile loam soil. Propagate by seed and division. Cutting stems to the ground after flowers are faded will promote repeat bloom during cool weather.

USES: Mixed beds and borders. Excellent for cutting. Powdered petals are a source of the natural organic insecticide Pyrethrum.

THALICTRUM AQUILEGIFOLIUM

COMMON NAME: Meadow rue, pink meadow rue

FAMILY: Ranunculaceae (Buttercups)

DESCRIPTION: Native to Europe and Asia. Plants form mounded clumps of lacy, blue-green leaves resembling columbine and tall stems topped with large flower clusters that resemble cotton candy. Early summer-flowering.

HEIGHT: 3 to 4 feet (.9 to 1.2m).

COLOR: Pink.

HARDINESS: Zones 5 to 9.

CULTURE: Grows in sun or light shade; needs well-drained, fertile, humus-rich soil. Propagate by division.

USES: Good tall accent in the back of beds and borders.

THALICTRUM SPECIOSISSIMUM

COMMON NAME: Meadow rue, yellow meadow rue

FAMILY: Ranunculaceae (Buttercups)

DESCRIPTION: Native to southern Europe. Plants grow clumps of tall flower spikes with oval, serrated, blue-green leaflets and tight, mounded, fluffy flower clusters. Summer-flowering.

HEIGHT: To 6 feet (1.8m).

COLOR: Yellow.

HARDINESS: Zones 5 to 9.

CULTURE: Prefers full sun, well-drained loam soil. Propagate by division. Generally needs staking to keep the flowers erect.

USES: Good tall accent in the back of mixed beds and borders.

THERMOPSIS CAROLINIANA

COMMON NAME: Carolina lupine, Aaron's red

FAMILY: Leguminosae (Peas)

DESCRIPTION: Native to the coastal Carolinas. Lupinelike plants form bushy clumps and spirelike clusters of pea flowers. Leaves are divided into three leaflets. Early summer-flowering.

HEIGHT: 3 to 4 feet (.9 to 1.2m).

COLOR: Yellow.

HARDINESS: Zones 3 to 8.

CULTURE: Prefers full sun, rich, light soil with good drainage; tolerates poor, infertile, sandy soil. Propagate by fresh seed and division.

USES: Tall accent in beds and borders.

TIARELLA CORDIFOLIA

COMMON NAME: Foamflower

FAMILY: Saxifragaceae (Saxifrages)

DESCRIPTION: Native to North America. Plants form spreading clumps of ivylike pale green leaves and lovely, tight flower spikes held above the foliage. Spring-flowering.

HEIGHT: 12 inches (31cm).

COLOR: White, sometimes tinged pink.

HARDINESS: Zones 5 to 9.

CULTURE: Prefers partial shade, moist, humus-rich sandy or loam soil. Propagate by division.

USES: Excellent for massing under trees in woodland wildflower gardens; edging rustic paths.

***TRADESCANTIA* × *ANDERSONIANA* (also *T. VIRGINIANA*)**

COMMON NAME: Spiderwort

FAMILY: Commelinaceae (Spiderworts)

DESCRIPTION: Hybrid of species native to North America. Plants form dense clumps of slender, arching, sword-shaped green leaves and 2-inch (5cm), triangular, three-petaled flowers. Early summer-flowering.

HEIGHT: To 2½ feet (.8m).

COLOR: Shades of blue, red, purple.

HARDINESS: Zones 5 to 9.

CULTURE: Prefers full sun or light shade; tolerates poor soil providing drainage is good. Propagate by division and stem cuttings.

USES: Accent in mixed beds and borders.

TRICYRTIS HIRTA

COMMON NAME: Toad lily

FAMILY: Liliaceae (Lilies)

DESCRIPTION: Native to Japan. Bushy plants have arching fountainlike stems crowded with smooth, lancelike, green leaves. The 1-inch (2.5cm), orchidlike flowers are borne in loose clusters on delicate branching stems. Late summer-flowering.

HEIGHT: To 3 feet (.9m).

COLOR: Pink with dark spots.

HARDINESS: Zones 4 to 9.

CULTURE: Prefers partial shade, moist, fertile, humus-rich sandy or loam soil. Propagate by division.

USES: Unusual accent in shade gardens.

TROLLIUS EUROPAEUS

COMMON NAME: Globeflower

FAMILY: Ranunculaceae (Buttercups)

DESCRIPTION: Native to Europe. Plants form clumps of feathery, bright green foliage. Slender, erect stems are topped with shimmering 2-inch (5cm), globular flowers. Spring-flowering.

HEIGHT: 2 to 2½ feet (.6 to .8m).

COLOR: Yellow.

HARDINESS: Zones 5 to 8.

CULTURE: Grows in sun or light shade; prefers cool, moist, humus-rich soil. Propagate by seed or division.

USES: Popular along stream banks and pond margins.

TYPHA LATIFOLIA

COMMON NAME: Broad-leaved cattail

FAMILY: Typhaceae (Cattails)

DESCRIPTION: Native to North America, Europe, and Asia. Colony-forming plants grow slender, reedlike stems; long, grasslike green leaves; and a poker-like flower cluster. Summer-flowering.

HEIGHT: To 6 feet (1.8m).

COLOR: Brown.

HARDINESS: Zones 4 to 9.

CULTURE: Prefers full sun, swampy soil, with roots permanently immersed in water. Propagate by root division.

USES: Popular in bog gardens and the margins of pools. Good companion to purple loosestrife. Suitable for coastal gardens.

VERBASCUM CHAIXII

COMMON NAME: Mullein, chaix mullein

FAMILY: Scrophulariaceae (Figworts)

DESCRIPTION: Native to Europe. Plants grow clumps of broad, spear-shaped, dark green leaves. Slender, erect flower spikes are studded with ½-inch (13mm) single flowers. Early summer-flowering.

HEIGHT: To 3 feet (.9m).

COLOR: White or pale yellow with reddish eye.

HARDINESS: Zones 5 to 9.

CULTURE: Prefers full sun, well-drained sandy or loam soil. Propagate by division or by seed direct-sown in spring.

USES: A vertical accent in mixed beds and borders.

VERBASCUM OLYMPICUM

COMMON NAME: Mullein, giant mullein

FAMILY: Scrophulariaceae (Figworts)

DESCRIPTION: Native to southern Europe. Plants form rosettes of broad, spear-shaped, woolly, silvery leaves and immense flower spikes that produce masses of flowers in a candelabra effect. Early summer-flowering.

HEIGHT: 6 to 8 feet (1.8 to 2.4m).

COLOR: Yellow.

HARDINESS: Zones 7 to 9.

CULTURE: Prefers full sun, well-drained soil; tolerates poor, infertile soil. Propagate by division.

USES: Tall accent in the back of beds and borders.

VERBENA PATAGONICA (also *V. BONARIENSIS*)

COMMON NAME: Vervain, candelabra verbena

FAMILY: Verbenaceae (Verbenas)

DESCRIPTION: Native to South America. Plants are full-branching with small, lance-like, dark green leaves and masses of flower clusters held high on slender stems. Summer-flowering.

HEIGHT: To 6 feet (1.8m).

COLOR: Purple.

HARDINESS: Zones 7 to 10. This tender perennial can be grown as an annual in colder zones.

CULTURE: Prefers full sun, well-drained sandy or loam soil. Best to propagate from seed started early indoors and transplant after danger of frost to flower the first year.

USES: Good tall accent in the back of mixed beds and borders.

VERBENA RIGIDA

COMMON NAME: Vervain

FAMILY: Verbenaceae (Verbenas)

DESCRIPTION: Native to South America. Low, spreading plants grow slender, toothed, lancelike, blue-green leaves and small florets arranged in a tight 1-inch (2.5cm) clustered circle. Summer-flowering.

HEIGHT: 18 inches (46cm).

COLOR: Purple.

HARDINESS: Zones 4 to 9.

CULTURE: Prefers full sun, well-drained sandy or loam soil; tolerates heat, drought. Propagate by seed, cuttings, division.

USES: Edging beds and borders.

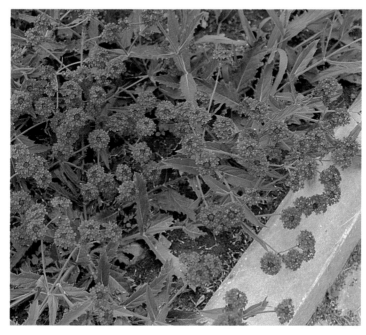

VERONICA LATIFOLIA

COMMON NAME: Speedwell, Hungarian speedwell

FAMILY: Scrophulariaceae (Figworts)

DESCRIPTION: Native to Europe. Plants form clumps of erect stems with spear-shaped, dark green leaves and tapering flower spikes. Late spring- and early summer-flowering; best during cool nights.

HEIGHT: 1½ to 2 feet (.5 to .6m).

COLOR: Blue.

HARDINESS: Zones 4 to 8.

CULTURE: Prefers full sun, good drainage; tolerates poor soil. Propagate by division.

USES: Good accent in mixed beds and borders.

VERONICA SPICATA

COMMON NAME: Speedwell, common speedwell

FAMILY: Scrophulariaceae (Figworts)

DESCRIPTION: Native to Europe and Asia. Plants form clumps of erect stems and spear-shaped green leaves with tapering flower spikes. Early summer-flowering.

HEIGHT: 2 feet (.6m).

COLOR: Blue, white, red, pink.

HARDINESS: Zones 4 to 8.

CULTURE: Prefers full sun, well-drained soil; thrives in poor, infertile soil. Propagate by division.

USES: Accent in mixed beds and borders.

VIOLA ODORATA

COMMON NAME: Sweet violet

FAMILY: Violaceae (Violets)

DESCRIPTION: Native to Europe. Plants form low, mounded clumps of heart-shaped, dark green leaves and fragrant ¾-inch (2cm), pansylike flowers. Early spring-flowering, continuous while nights are cool.

HEIGHT: 6 to 8 inches (15 to 20cm).

COLOR: Blue.

HARDINESS: Zones 4 to 8.

CULTURE: Grows in sun or light shade; prefers humus-rich, well-drained loam soil. Propagate by seed and division.

USES: Edging paths, beds, borders; massing under trees as a ground cover.

YUCCA FILAMENTOSA

COMMON NAME: Adam's-needle

FAMILY: Agavaceae (Agaves)

DESCRIPTION: Native to arid areas of the United States. Plants form clumps of stiff, spiky dark green leaves tipped with sharp spines. From the center of each clump arises a strong stem topped with a candelabralike cluster of nodding, cup-shaped flowers to 2 inches (5cm) long. Summer-flowering.

HEIGHT: 4 to 5 feet (1.2 to 1.5m).

COLOR: Waxy white.

HARDINESS: Zones 5 to 10.

CULTURE: Prefers full sun, good drainage; thrives even in poor, impoverished soil. Does best where summers are warm and sunny. Propagate from offsets, which appear around the mother plant.

USES: Accent in mixed beds and borders. Excellent for erosion control on dry slopes.

HARDINESS ZONE MAP

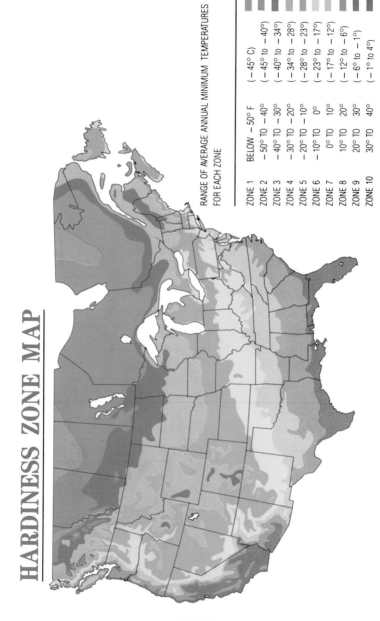

RANGE OF AVERAGE ANNUAL MINIMUM TEMPERATURES
FOR EACH ZONE

ZONE 1	BELOW −50° F	(−45° C)
ZONE 2	−50° TO −40°	(−45° to −40°)
ZONE 3	−40° TO −30°	(−40° to −34°)
ZONE 4	−30° TO −20°	(−34° to −28°)
ZONE 5	−20° TO −10°	(−28° to −23°)
ZONE 6	−10° TO 0°	(−23° to −17°)
ZONE 7	0° TO 10°	(−17° to −12°)
ZONE 8	10° TO 20°	(−12° to −6°)
ZONE 9	20° TO 30°	(−6° to −1°)
ZONE 10	30° TO 40°	(−1° to 4°)

INDEX